PIEDMONT

TRAVEL GUIDE

2024

Land of the Savoy Hills: Navigating The Uncharted

Terrain

RYDER . D. WHELAN

Disclaimer

The information contained in this document is intended for entertainment and educational purposes only, and should not be construed as proficient advice. While every effort has been made to ensure its accuracy and completeness, no warranties are implied. Readers acknowledge that the author is not responsible for any direct or indirect losses incurred as a result of using the information contained within this document.

CONTENTS

INTRODUCTION

Commencing my odyssey in the historic city of Turin, I was greeted by a tapestry of grandeur and refinement at every corner. Wandering through the labyrinthine cobblestone streets, I found myself enraptured by the opulent palaces, intricate churches, and lively piazzas that whispered tales of a bygone era. The Royal Palace of Venaria, with its expansive gardens and regal halls, stood as a testament to the magnificence of the House of Savoy, evoking a profound sense of awe within me.

Yet, it was within the hidden enclaves of Turin that I discovered the true essence of Piedmont. Serendipitously stumbling upon quaint cafes adorned with the aroma of rich espresso and delectable pastries, I witnessed the camaraderie of locals exchanging stories and laughter. Venturing into the Quadrilatero Romano district, I embarked on a journey through narrow alleys adorned with artisanal boutiques and quaint shops, unearthing bespoke treasures and mementos to cherish for eternity.

Leaving the urban tapestry behind, I traversed into the picturesque countryside, where vineyards sprawled across the landscape as far as the eye could see. Immersed in the splendor of the Langhe region, I indulged in immersive wine tasting experiences, relishing the intricate nuances of Barolo, Barbaresco, and Barbera wines. Each sip was a revelation, a voyage through the terroir of Piedmont, an ode to the dedication and passion of its vintners.

Further exploration led me to encounter the natural marvels of Piedmont, from the serene shores of Lake Orta to the rugged peaks of the Alps. Trekking through lush valleys and ascending to lofty vantage points, I was mesmerized by panoramic vistas that stirred my soul. Upon reaching the idyllic village of Orta San Giulio, I embarked on a tranquil boat ride to the enchanting island of San Giulio, where ancient churches and verdant gardens provided solace for contemplation and introspection.

However, it was the warmth and hospitality of the people of Piedmont that etched unforgettable memories into my journey. Sharing communal meals with local families, I savored the exquisite flavors of Piedmontese cuisine, from the delicate agnolotti pasta to the succulent vitello tonnato and velvety risottos. Each gastronomic delight was a homage to the region's culinary heritage, a symphony of tastes and textures that danced upon my palate.

One evening, amidst the bustling town of Alba, I found myself engulfed in the intoxicating aroma of truffles. Amidst the fervor of truffle season, I joined fellow enthusiasts in a quest for the elusive white truffle, guided by seasoned hunters and their faithful companions. As we traversed through the dense forests in pursuit of treasure, I felt an intimate connection with the land and its abundant offerings.

As my sojourn through Piedmont drew to a close, I realized that I had embarked upon more than a mere voyage – it was a transformative expedition. Amidst the splendor of Piedmont's landscapes, the cultural richness, and the heartfelt warmth of its inhabitants, I discovered inspiration, joy, and a rekindled sense of wonder. And as I bid farewell to this enchanting land, I knew that the memories forged would forever remain ingrained in my heart.

SCAN THE QRCODE TO SEE PIEDMONT MAP

History and Heritage

The origins and etymology of "Piedmont" offer a glimpse into its linguistic evolution. Tracing back to medieval Latin, the term "Pedemontium" or "Pedemontis" translates to "at the foot of the mountains," eloquently encapsulating the region's geographical proximity to the majestic Alps. Referred to as "Piemonte" in Italian and "Piemont" in Piedmontese, the name resonates with the region's intrinsic connection to its mountainous surroundings.

Geographically, Piedmont finds itself embraced on three sides by the towering Alps, with notable peaks such as Monviso, the source of the iconic Po River, and the majestic Monte Rosa gracing its landscape. Sharing borders with France, Switzerland, and neighboring Italian regions like Lombardy, Liguria, Aosta Valley, and Emilia-Romagna, Piedmont emerges as a cultural crossroads, enriched by diverse influences.

Piedmont's cultural heritage is deeply intertwined with its illustrious past. As the cradle of the House of Savoy, a formidable dynasty pivotal in the unification of Italy, Piedmont boasts architectural marvels like the Royal Palace of Turin, serving as enduring symbols of dynastic power and influence. Additionally, the region's culinary prowess shines through its renowned wines, including the esteemed Barolo, Barbaresco, and Asti Spumante, while annual events like the White Truffle Fair in Alba draw gourmands and epicureans from far and wide.

The artistic and architectural splendor of Piedmont finds expression in its capital, Turin, home to prestigious museums like the Egyptian Museum and the National Cinema Museum. The iconic Mole Antonelliana stands tall as a testament to the region's architectural ingenuity and cultural significance.

Piedmont's literary legacy is equally illustrious, boasting luminaries like Umberto Eco, author of the acclaimed "The Name of the Rose," and Primo Levi, whose poignant works reflect his experiences as a Holocaust survivor during World War II.

The region's industrial heritage is exemplified by landmarks such as FIAT, the renowned automobile manufacturer founded in Turin, and the historic Lingotto Factory, once a bustling hub of car production and now repurposed into a multifaceted complex featuring a shopping center, hotel, and exhibition spaces.

Nature's bounty adds to Piedmont's allure, with the picturesque Langhe Hills, a UNESCO World Heritage site renowned for its rolling vineyards and quaint villages, and the serene beauty of Lake Maggiore, a breathtaking alpine oasis shared with Switzerland, adorned with charming islands that beckon travelers to explore and unwind.

Thus, exploring Piedmont unveils a multifaceted tapestry of history, culture, and natural splendor, offering an enriching and unforgettable experience for all who journey through its captivating landscapes.

Geography and Climate

Geography: Piedmont, holding the distinction of being the second-largest region in Italy by land area, occupies the northwestern swath of the country. Its coastal boundaries are separated from direct access to the sea by the Ligurian Apennine range.

To the west and north, Piedmont is enclosed by the formidable Alps, delineating its natural borders. Notably, these include the Maritimes, Cottian, and Graian Alps along the border with France, as well as the Pennine and Lepontine Alps bordering the Valle d'Aosta region and Switzerland. Serving as a protective shield, the Alps safeguard Piedmont from cold air invasions originating in the north and cool, humid winds sweeping in from France.

At times, however, the winds manage to surmount the mountain ridges, resulting in the manifestation of the föhn, a warm, dry wind capable of significantly elevating temperatures even during the winter months. While the Apennine range, though lower in altitude, does not entirely deter rains from the Ligurian Sea, it does impede southerly winds at lower elevations. Amidst the expansive flatlands, rolling hills grace the landscape, including the Po Hills near Turin and the Langhe, Roero, and Monferrat Hills to the southeast.

Additionally, picturesque lakes such as Lake Maggiore, shared with Lombardy and the Canton of Ticino, and Lake Orta, nestled amidst the landscape, further enhance the natural beauty of Piedmont. The Po River, originating from Monviso, meanders gracefully through the region's capital, Turin, positioned at an altitude of 250 meters (820 feet).

Climate: Piedmont's diverse topography gives rise to a range of climatic conditions. The mountainous western and northern areas, including the Alps, experience a cold mountain climate, while the northern Pre-Alps and southern Apennines offer a temperate humid climate.

Occasionally, the Alpine and pre-Alpine valleys are graced by the föhn, which brings clear skies and excellent visibility. In contrast, the central-eastern part of Piedmont, encompassing the Po Valley, features a semi-continental climate, characterized by relatively cold winters and hot, muggy summers.

Rainfall distribution varies across the region, with the northern Pre-Alps receiving abundant precipitation exceeding 2,000 millimeters (80 inches) annually, while the southernmost areas on the Ligurian Apennines also experience heavy rainfall. Conversely, the southeastern plain, including the provinces of Asti and Alessandria, receives less rain, with precipitation dropping below 650 mm (25.5 inches) per year.

Mountains and Ski Resorts: Piedmont's mountainous terrain is home to a plethora of ski resorts, including Sestriere, Bardonecchia, and Alagna Valsesia. Sestriere, perched at an elevation of 2,035 meters (6,675 feet) in the province of Turin, showcases a diverse range of temperatures throughout the year. In December 1996, temperatures plummeted to -21°C (-6°F), while in August 2003, they soared to 26°C (79°F), offering a testament to the region's climatic variability.

Getting Around Piedmont

BY CAR

Optimal Mode of Transport: Renting a car provides the utmost convenience for exploring Piedmont. With your own vehicle, you can venture into the countryside, meander through charming villages, and uncover hidden treasures that may be inaccessible by public transportation.

Road Infrastructure: Piedmont boasts a well-established road network, seamlessly connecting major urban centers and scenic routes that traverse rolling hills and vineyard-draped landscapes, adding to the allure of your journey.

Car Rental Services: Renting a car affords you the flexibility to craft your own itinerary and traverse the region at your preferred pace.

BY TRAIN

Reliable Rail System: Piedmont's train network is robust and dependable, facilitating seamless connectivity between key destinations. Opting for train travel not only offers a convenient mode of transportation but also aligns with eco-friendly principles.

Turin Hub: The capital city, Turin, serves as a pivotal nexus for train travel within Piedmont, serving as a launching pad for exploring other enchanting locales in the region.

PRIVATE DRIVER

Engage a Personal Driver: If self-driving isn't your preference, consider hiring a private driver. A dedicated chauffeur can chauffeur you to wineries, picturesque hamlets, and noteworthy attractions, eliminating the stress of navigating unfamiliar roads.

E-BIKES:

E-Bike Rentals: For an active and environmentally conscious excursion, consider renting e-bikes. Embark on scenic rides through vineyard-laden landscapes, relish the crisp mountain air, and pedal your way through the Langhe region, renowned for producing some of Italy's finest wines.

EXPLORING ATTRACTIONS IN PIEDMONT'S MAJOR CITIES

Turin: The Royal Capital

1. **Egyptian Museum (Museo Egizio):** Located on Accademia delle Scienze Street, the Egyptian Museum houses a rich collection of ancient Egyptian artifacts, including mummies, papyri, statues, and other archaeological wonders. Among its notable features are replicas of the Rosetta Stone, crucial in deciphering hieroglyphs, and a meticulously reconstructed version of Tutankhamun's Tomb, adorned with intricate details. The museum operates daily from 9:00 AM to 6:30 PM, with closure on Mondays at 2:00 PM.

2. **Mole Antonelliana:** The Mole Antonelliana, an iconic structure in Turin's skyline, originally conceived as a synagogue, now houses the National Museum of Cinema, offering visitors a cinematic journey through engaging exhibits, vintage film apparatus, and iconic movie paraphernalia.

Ascend via elevator to enjoy panoramic vistas of the cityscape and the majestic Alps, with operating hours from 9:00 AM to 8:00 PM daily, and extended hours on Saturdays.

3. **Royal Palace of Turin (Palazzo Reale):** The historical abode of the House of Savoy, Italy's royal lineage, boasts opulent interiors adorned with resplendent chambers, extravagant furnishings, and distinguished art compilations. Visitors can explore the expansive armory, which showcases an array of armor, weaponry, and ceremonial garb, and then meander through the exquisite Royal Gardens adjoining the palace. Operating hours vary according to seasons, so it's advisable to refer to the official website for precise details.

4. **Piazza Castello:** Piazza Castello stands as the central hub of Turin, surrounded by historic edifices that exude timeless charm.

Witness the captivating fusion of medieval and baroque architectural styles at Palazzo Madama, now home to the Civic Museum of Ancient Art. Adorning the square is the regal Teatro Regio, an opulent opera house that adds a touch of grandeur to the surroundings. Indulge in Turin's famed café culture as you savor a cup of coffee at one of the quaint cafés, immersing yourself in the vibrant ambiance that permeates the square.

5. **Basilica of Superga (Basilica di Superga):** Nestled atop the Superga Hill, this hilltop sanctuary offers breathtaking panoramas of Turin and the winding Po River. Marvel at the resplendent baroque architecture and intricately frescoed dome, which exude timeless elegance. Experience a nostalgic journey aboard the Sassi-Superga tramway to reach this historical gem, adding to the allure of the visit. Within the basilica's confines, discover the sepulchers of illustrious members of the House of Savoy, enriching the experience with a sense of historical significance.

➤ *SAN GAUDENZIO BASILICA*

Majestic Edifice: The San Gaudenzio Basilica stands prominently at the heart of Novara, with its remarkable dome soaring towards the heavens.

Rich Heritage: With roots dating back to the 16th century, this basilica encapsulates centuries of history and religious devotion, a testament to the enduring legacy of its construction spanning multiple generations.

Sweeping Scenery: Ascend the spiral staircase to the apex of the dome, where breathtaking vistas of Novara and its surrounding panorama unfold before your eyes.

Location: Via Carlo Bescape 16, Novara, NO, 28100 .

➢ MIRASOLE CASTLE-FARM

Located in Strada Provinciale 229, Località Mirasole, the neighboring town of Caltignaga, the Mirasole Castle-Farm captures the rustic charm of a farmhouse dating back to the 15th century. Surrounded by lush fields and tranquil greenery, this lovingly restored castle-farm offers a serene setting, providing a glimpse into both rural life and architectural legacy. Visitors can wander through its delightful courtyards, marvel at the time-worn walls steeped in history, and immerse themselves in the ambiance of past eras.

➢ *IL BROLETTO*

Historical Residence: Il Broletto, also recognized as the Palace of the Paratici, stands as an architectural marvel.

Architectural Harmony: Its exterior showcases a graceful blend of medieval and baroque influences, characterized by layered arches that narrate tales of bygone eras.

Cultural Hub: Within Il Broletto, visitors can explore an art gallery showcasing the talents of local artists. Following an enriching art experience, unwind at the charming café nestled within the palace precincts.

> ## CATHEDRAL OF SANTA MARIA ASSUNTA

The Cathedral of Santa Maria Assunta stands as a prominent emblem of Novara's religious heritage. Inside, visitors are treated to captivating tombs, a beautifully embellished altar, and remarkable architectural details. Despite its modest elegance, the cathedral's simplicity holds a distinctive charm. You can find it at Piazza della Repubblica, Novara, NO, 28100.

Asti: City of Festivals

Torre Troyana

Location and Historical Importance: Situated in the picturesque Piazza Medici, Torre Troyana stands tall as a medieval tower, once an integral part of Asti's defensive fortifications. Today, it serves as a poignant symbol of Asti's illustrious past.

Panoramic Views: Ascend to the tower's summit for awe-inspiring panoramic vistas, showcasing the city's charming streets and sprawling vineyards.

Contact Information: You can find Torre Troyana at Piazza Medici 6, Asti, AT, 14100.

Agrilatteria Del Pianalto

Rustic Charm and Farm-to-Table Experience: Located in the scenic outskirts of Valfenera, Agrilatteria Del Pianalto offers an authentic agriturismo experience, allowing visitors to savor locally-produced cheeses, wines, and other farm-fresh delights.

Scenic Surroundings: Surrounded by rolling hills and lush vineyards, the agriturismo provides a serene setting for relaxation and immersion in nature's beauty.

Location: You can visit Agrilatteria Del Pianalto at Strada Valmaggiore, 2, Valfenera, AT, 14017.

Basilica di San Gaudenzio

Impressive Architecture and Historical Legacy: Asti's skyline is graced by the majestic cupola of the Basilica di San Gaudenzio, a testament to the city's rich architectural heritage. Dating back to the 16th century, this basilica houses invaluable art and relics, offering a glimpse into centuries of history.

Spectacular Views: Climb the spiral staircase within the basilica to enjoy breathtaking panoramic views of Asti and its scenic surroundings.

Location: You can find Basilica di San Gaudenzio at Via Carlo Bescape 16, Novara, NO, 28100.

Il Broletto

Historical Palace and Art Gallery: Il Broletto, also known as the Palace of the Paratici, stands as a splendid example of medieval and baroque architecture in Asti. Within its walls, an art gallery showcases the works of local artists, providing a delightful cultural experience.

Relaxing Café Atmosphere: Unwind at the cozy café nestled within Il Broletto, where you can bask in the ambiance of Asti's rich history while enjoying a refreshing beverage.

Cattedrale di Santa Maria Assunta

Religious Significance: The Cathedral of Santa Maria Assunta stands as a beacon of religious devotion in Novara, reflecting the city's deep spiritual heritage.

Intriguing Interior: Explore the cathedral's interior to discover fascinating tombs, an intricately adorned altar, and architectural marvels that tell the story of Novara's past.

Location: You can visit the Cattedrale di Santa Maria Assunta at Piazza della Repubblica, Novara, NO, 28100.

Alessandria: Historic Crossroads

1. The Citadel of Alessandria: The Citadel, an impressive feat of engineering, stands as a historic fortification with a commanding presence. Originally built for defense, it now serves as a symbol of the city's vibrant history. It is located at Strada Provinciale Pavia, 2, Alessandria, Piedmont, 15121.

2. Borsalino Hat Museum: The museum presents a distinctive exhibition featuring a variety of beautiful hats crafted in Borsalino's factory.

Visitors can delve into the intricate craftsmanship and artistic expression behind these iconic headpieces. Located at Corso Acqui, 77, Alessandria, Piedmont, 15121.

3. **Saint Peter's Cathedral:** The cathedral, a sacred landmark, commands attention with its towering spire that overlooks the cityscape. Within, the baroque interior creates a tranquil ambiance.

Situated at Piazza San Pietro, Alessandria, Piedmont, 15121.

4. Cittadella Bridge: The Cittadella Bridge, a historic crossing over the Tanaro River, links the city with its graceful arches and scenic vistas.

Situated along the Tanaro River in Alessandria, Piedmont, 15121.

5. **Military Uniform Museum:** Delve into the insightful collection showcasing the history of military uniforms and artifacts, uncovering the stories of those who served,

located at Via Giuseppe Garibaldi, 1, Alessandria, Piedmont, 15121.

Biella: Wool and Textile Hub

✓ *Gromo Losa Palace*

Architectural Gem: Once an elegant noble dwelling, Gromo Losa Palace boasts a fascinating historical legacy.

Historical Development: Its northeastern section likely originates from the 14th century, while subsequent expansions have shaped its current form.

Cultural Center: Today, it serves as a vibrant exhibition space and a hub for social and cultural events.

Versatile Venue: With its charming and flexible spaces, it's an excellent location for conferences, meetings, and musical performances.

Italian Garden: The expansive private Italian garden, covering approximately 10,000 square meters, enhances the palace's allure.

✓ *Quartiere Del Piazzo*

Historic Quarter: Every cobblestone street and corner in Quartiere Del Piazzo resonates with tales of history and folklore.

Bridge Entry: Crossing the bridge into this district feels like stepping into a bygone era.

✓ *Veglio Adventure Park*

Thrilling Outdoor Experience: Veglio Adventure Park stands out as one of Italy's most scenic and comprehensive adventure destinations.

Enchanting Forest Setting: Nestled within a chestnut forest, it offers a variety of obstacles such as ladders, nets, swings, and zip-lines.

Courses for All Ages: Whether you're young or young at heart, the park provides courses suited to different skill levels.

✓ *San Gaudenzio Basilica*

Impressive Structure: San Gaudenzio Basilica boasts a remarkable dome that has become an iconic symbol of the city.

Rich Heritage: Dating back to the 16th century, the basilica houses a remarkable collection of ancient artworks and relics.

Panoramic Views: Climb the spiral staircase to enjoy breathtaking vistas of Biella and its surroundings.

✓ *Il Broletto*

Historic Dwelling: Il Broletto, also known as the Palace of the Paratici, showcases an intriguing blend of medieval and baroque architectural elements.

Artistic Hub: Explore the works of local artists displayed within the palace's art gallery.

Relaxing Ambiance: Take a moment to unwind in the cozy atmosphere of the café while immersing yourself in the area's rich historical ambiance.

Vercelli: Rice Capital of Italy

1. Basilica of Sant'Andrea: The basilica is a standout landmark in Vercelli, renowned for its captivating architecture and profound historical importance, rendering it an essential destination within the city. It is conveniently located within Vercelli.

2. Cathedral of Sant'Eusebio: The Cathedral of Sant'Eusebio stands as a testament to Vercelli's profound religious heritage, reflecting its deep-rooted faith.

Venture inside to discover captivating tombs, intricately adorned altars, and other remarkable architectural details. Situated at Piazza San Pietro, Vercelli.

3. Church of San Cristoforo:

Adorned Walls: Adorning the interior walls of this church are splendid frescoes by Gaudenzio Ferraris, a master of the Renaissance era.

Artistic Marvels: The detailed artwork enhances the church's appeal.

Location: Located within Vercelli.

4. Piazza Cavour

Vibrant Center: Piazza Cavour serves as a bustling focal point surrounded by historic edifices.

Palazzo Madama: Witness the harmonious blend of medieval and baroque architecture in Palazzo Madama, which now houses the Civic Museum of Ancient Art.

Royal Theatre: Adorning the square is the elegant Teatro Regio, adding to its cultural significance.

Cafés and Atmosphere: Indulge in a cup of coffee at one of the delightful cafés while immersing yourself in the lively ambiance.

5. Borgogna Museum

Specialized Exhibits: The Borgogna Museum showcases archaeological treasures and ancient art collections, shedding light on Vercelli's rich history and heritage.

Artistic Displays: Explore a curated selection of decorative art pieces, including majolica, glassware, and furniture.

Location: Positioned at Via Giuseppe Garibaldi, 1, Vercelli.

Cuneo: Gateway to the Western Alps

GALIMBERTI SQUARE: Galimberti Square in Cuneo serves as a significant boundary, separating the historic district focused around Via Roma from the more modern area situated along Corso Nizza. The square is distinguished by its covered walkways, which not only offer protection from the weather but also provide an inviting atmosphere for leisurely strolls. You can find Galimberti Square nestled within the city of Cuneo.

HISTORIC CENTER: Discover the delightful alleys of Cuneo's historic center, where each lane exudes its own unique charm. As you wander through these quaint alleyways, you'll find yourself immersed in the city's rich history and architectural wonders. Adding to the appeal of the exploration are the covered passageways known as arcades, which not only shield you from the elements but also offer a cozy atmosphere for leisurely walks.

These protected passageways ensure that you can enjoy your exploration of Cuneo's historic center in comfort, regardless of the weather conditions.

VALLE MAIRA: Experience the breathtaking beauty of Valle Maira, an idyllic valley that entices nature enthusiasts with its scenic splendor. Explore the abundant hiking opportunities, where you can traverse scenic trails, immerse yourself in the fresh air, and admire the stunning landscapes that unfold before you.

SAN FRANCESCO CHURCH: At San Francesco Church, marvel at the harmonious blend of artistry and architecture showcased through its fascinating tombs, ornate altar, and distinctive architectural elements. Enjoy complimentary admission to explore its treasures, with optional guided tours offered for a fee. You can find this historical gem nestled in Piazza San Pietro, Cuneo.

CIVIC TOWER: The Civic Tower is a symbol of Cuneo's rich history, offering sweeping panoramas from its summit that showcase the city and its surrounding areas. You can find this historical icon nestled within Cuneo

Ivrea: Historic Industrial Center

> ➢ Roman Bridge Museum

The museum in Pont-Saint-Martin offers a glimpse into Italy's industrial history, particularly focusing on the Olivetti legacy and culture. It serves a dual purpose, functioning both as a museum showcasing ancient artifacts and as a laboratory promoting creativity and experimentation. You can find it at Via Emile Chanoux, Pont-Saint-Martin, AO, 11026.

> ➢ The Donkey Sanctuary

In Sala Biellese, you'll find Il Rifugio degli Asinelli, a haven for rescued donkeys.

The sanctuary not only cares for these animals but also advocates for their welfare, aiming to raise awareness about their importance. You can locate it at Via per Zubiena, 62, Sala Biellese, BI, 13884.

> ➤ The Battle of Oranges

During the mid-winter carnival, Ivrea hosts an unconventional festival where the town turns into a battleground with participants hurling oranges. This historical reenactment commemorates a legendary fight for freedom from oppression. Nine teams representing different neighborhoods actively engage in the orange battle.

> ➤ Church of San Bernardino

San Bernardino Church in Ivrea is a historical site that showcases remarkable religious architecture. Inside, visitors can marvel at intricate frescoes and stunning architectural features that reflect centuries of devotion and artistic expression. It is located within the city of Ivrea.

> Cathedral of Santa Maria Assunta

The Cathedral of Santa Maria Assunta in Ivrea is a significant religious landmark, reflecting the city's deep religious devotion. Inside, visitors can discover fascinating tombs, an ornate altar, and other remarkable architectural features. It is situated in Piazza San Pietro, Ivrea.

Alba: Truffle Capital

1. Wine Tastings: Alba is celebrated for its exceptional wines. Explore local vineyards and savor wine tastings, particularly the renowned Barolo and Barbaresco varieties.

2. Truffle Hunting: Alba holds the title of Italy's truffle capital. Join a truffle hunting expedition and experience the excitement of uncovering these aromatic treasures alongside expertly trained dogs.

3. Historic Center: Take a leisurely stroll through the historic streets of Alba. Marvel at the medieval architecture, quaint squares, and hidden gems waiting to be discovered.

4. Alba Cathedral (Cattedrale di San Lorenzo): Explore the striking beauty of the Alba Cathedral, characterized by its distinctive red brick façade. Delve into its interior to admire the artistry and delve into its rich history.

5. Alba White Truffle Fair: If you're in Alba during autumn, be sure to attend the annual White Truffle Fair. Indulge in truffle-infused delicacies and immerse yourself in the culinary delights that Alba has to offer.

Mondovì: Charming Hilltop Town

Piazza Maggiore

Historical Square: Piazza Maggiore charms visitors with its vibrant atmosphere, where locals gather and visitors can soak in the lively ambiance.

Weekly Market: Every Friday morning, a bustling market offers a variety of local products, including cheese, vegetables, and more.

Torre del Belvedere

Panoramic Views & Gardens: Situated atop Monte Regale, Torre del Belvedere boasts panoramic vistas of Mondovì and its surroundings. Adjacent to the tower, Parco del Tempo features intriguing sundials and lush greenery.

Museo della Ceramica

Specialized Exhibition: Housed in Palazzo Fauzone di Germagnano, this museum is dedicated to ceramics, showcasing ancient artifacts and offering insights into the art of ceramic craftsmanship.

Visiting Hours: Open from Tuesday to Sunday, with varying hours.

Chiesa della Missione

Historic Religious Site: Dating back to the late 17th century, Chiesa della Missione impresses with its grand sandstone facade.

Artistic Delights: Inside, visitors can admire intricate frescoes and architectural elements that narrate centuries of history.

Duomo di San Donato

Religious Landmark: The Cathedral of San Donato exemplifies exquisite religious architecture.

Interior Marvels: Explore fascinating tombs, an ornate altar, and other architectural intricacies within the cathedral's walls.

NATURAL WONDERS

The Majestic Alps

1. Varied Alpine Regions

The Italian Alps encompass three distinct areas:

Western Alps: Nestled along the southern border with France and Switzerland, this region boasts snow-capped peaks and rugged terrain.

Central Alps: The Italian Lakes region showcases expansive lakes surrounded by gentle hills and quaint villages.

Eastern Alps (Dolomites): Characterized by jagged rocky spires and verdant alpine meadows, this area presents a unique and dramatic landscape.

Tre Cime di Lavaredo

Among the world's most iconic mountain formations, Tre Cime di Lavaredo comprises three imposing peaks side by side, offering accessible trails and awe-inspiring vistas along the Tre Cime hike. Along the route, mountain huts provide refreshments and delectable Italian cuisine.

Lago di Braies (Pragser Wildsee)

Lago di Braies, or Pragser Wildsee, boasts a breathtaking alpine lake encircled by forested slopes and rugged summits. Its crystal-clear waters mirror the glacial radiance, creating a magical ambiance for visitors.

Seceda Ridgeline: Traverse the Seceda ridgeline in the Dolomites, immersing yourself in the splendor of the Italian Mountains while enjoying panoramic vistas of the surrounding valleys and peaks beneath sheer vertical cliffs.

Lake Como:

Lake Como, nestled amidst the foothills of the Alps, captivates with its grace and natural allure, inviting you to explore charming lakeside towns, historic villas, and lush gardens dotting the shores of this glacial lake.

The Italian Alps beckon visitors year-round, offering summer hiking and winter skiing opportunities. Whether you're an outdoor enthusiast, a photography enthusiast, or simply seeking serenity, the Italian Alps guarantee an unforgettable journey.

Picturesque Lakes and Rivers

LAKE MAGGIORE

Borromeo Islands Archipelago: Lake Maggiore is adorned with the exquisite Borromean Islands—Isola Madre, Isola Bella, and Isola dei Pescatori.

Picturesque Views: Experience enchanting vistas in the gulf near Stresa, where these islands form a mesmerizing backdrop.

LAKE MERGOZZO

Hidden Gem: Lake Mergozzo is a delightful find, bordered by charming lakeside resorts.

Tranquil Serenity: Its pristine waters and peaceful ambiance make it a perfect spot for relaxation.

LAKE ORTA

Enchanting Atmosphere: Lake Orta is cloaked in allure and intrigue.

San Giulio Island: Explore San Giulio Island, home to a majestic Basilica—one of Piedmont's significant Romanesque landmarks.

Lakes of Viverone and Mucrone

Biella Region: Uncover the serene Lakes of Viverone and Mucrone in the Biella area.

Natural Parks: Venture into the nearby Nature Parks of Lake Candia and the Lakes of Avigliana on the outskirts of Turin.

Piedmont's lakes and rivers present a vibrant spectrum of colors, from myriad shades of green to the deepest blues. Each body of water possesses its own charm, beckoning travelers to immerse themselves in the splendor of nature.

Verdant Valleys and Hillsides

1. Langhe Region: Explore the Langhe region's scenic terrain, where vineyards, fruit orchards, and quaint villages create a picturesque tapestry. This wine country is famed for its Barolo and Barbaresco wines, cultivated amidst the rolling hills. Delight in envisioning the grapes destined for future bottles as you embark on truffle-hunting excursions in mist-covered forests, immersing yourself in a sensory journey deeply rooted in the earth.

2. Lake Maggiore: Experience the tranquility of Lake Maggiore, where serene waters are embraced by verdant hills, shared with Switzerland.

Explore the enchanting Borromean Islands—Isola Madre, Isola Bella, and Isola dei Pescatori—each boasting its own unique charm and historical significance, adding to the allure of this picturesque destination.

Lake Orta: Discover the hidden sanctuary of Lake Orta, often overshadowed by its larger counterparts, yet offering a serene oasis of tranquility. Step foot on the enchanting San Giulio Island, where a basilica presides over cobblestone pathways and ancient edifices, adding to the island's captivating allure.

Monferrato Hills: Indulge in the rural serenity of the Monferrato hills, where a tranquil panorama of vineyards, hazelnut orchards, and golden wheat fields unfolds. Explore the medieval charms of towns like Saluzzo and Neive, where labyrinthine streets wind among rustic dwellings, inviting you to wander and discover their timeless allure.

Valle Maira: Embark on a journey through the primal wilderness of Valle Maira, a hidden treasure revealing soaring peaks, glacial valleys, and a rich tapestry of wildlife. Whether you crave leisurely strolls or challenging hikes, the trails of Valle Maira offer a hiking haven, promising endless exploration and adventure for all who venture into its embrace.

Enchanting National Parks

GRAN PARADISO NATIONAL PARK

Spanning both the Aosta Valley and Piedmont regions, this wildlife sanctuary is home to diverse flora and fauna, including ibex, chamois, and golden eagles, amidst its scenic beauty of alpine meadows, glaciers, and rugged peaks.

LAGHI DI AVIGLIANA NATIONAL PARK

Surrounding the enchanting Lakes of Avigliana, this area offers a plethora of outdoor activities such as hiking, birdwatching, and picnics amidst lush greenery. For breathtaking panoramic views of the lakes and surrounding hills, climb Monte Pirchiriano.

PARCO NAZIONALE DELLA VAL GRANDE

Wilderness Experience: Italy's largest wilderness area beckons with untamed beauty, inviting you to explore rugged terrain, dense forests, and pristine rivers along hiking trails that traverse ancient chestnut groves and lead to hidden valleys.

RISERVA NATURALE CRAVA MOROZZO

Renowned for its rich biodiversity, this reserve offers opportunities to encounter unique plant species and observe wildlife in their natural habitat.

OASI WWF BARAGGIA DI BELLINZAGO

Serving as a protector of wetlands and a supporter of migratory birds, this location also functions as an educational center where visitors can learn about environmental conservation and the significance of wetland ecosystems.

Mountains and beaches

1. Gran Paradiso National Park:

- Situated in both the Aosta Valley and Piedmont regions.
- Abode to a variety of flora and fauna, including ibex, chamois, and golden eagles.
- Wander through alpine meadows, glaciers, and rugged peaks.

2. Langhe Region

> ➤ Dotted with rolling hills adorned with vineyards, orchards, and picturesque villages.

> ➤ Renowned for producing exceptional wines such as Barolo and Barbaresco.

> ➤ Delight in truffle hunting and wine tasting experiences.

3. Lake Maggiore

> ✓ Tranquil waters embraced by verdant hills.

> ✓ Explore the enchanting Borromean Islands—Isola Madre, Isola Bella, and Isola dei Pescatori.

Beaches

Felizzano Beach: Discovered in Felizzano, Alessandria, this beach invites visitors to unwind and absorb the tranquil lakeside ambiance. You can locate it at Strada Padana 10 Ovest 3, Felizzano, AL, 15023. For inquiries, please dial +349 101 5893 .

Spiaggia Miami: The beach and pool club provide a delightful lakeside retreat where visitors can indulge in the restaurant, relax on comfortable beds, and enjoy a water slide.

Asti Lido 2000 Piscine: Located on the outskirts of Asti, this fantastic waterpark offers pools and leisure facilities, making it an ideal destination for families in search of a fun-filled day.

Lido Di Cannero: Nestled on the western shore of Lake Maggiore, this spot invites you to unwind on its sandy beach and immerse yourself in the crystal-clear waters. Don't forget to explore the nearby medieval castle and the charming town of Cannero Riviera.

Natural Baay - Lido di Gozzano: Experience the serenity of Lake Orta while embracing cherished moments with your loved ones by the lakeside.

CULINARY DELIGHTS

Gastronomic Traditions

TRUFFLES: Famous for its truffles, especially the highly sought-after white truffle from Alba, Piedmont is renowned worldwide. Truffle festivals honor this earthy delicacy, showcasing its richness in dishes such as pasta, risotto, and eggs. Immerse yourself in the alluring aroma and exquisite flavor of truffle-infused cuisine.

WINES: Piedmont is a paradise for wine lovers, boasting renowned varieties such as Barolo, Barbaresco, and Barbera. The Nebbiolo grape flourishes in this region, yielding robust red wines characterized by nuanced flavors. Embark on vineyard explorations, winery tours, and indulge in the distinctive terroir of Piedmontese wines.

HAZELNUTS AND GIANDUIA: Turin, the capital of Piedmont, is credited with introducing gianduia—a delightful hazelnut chocolate spread. Nutella, beloved worldwide, traces its roots back to gianduia, emerging during the cocoa shortages of the 19th century. Indulge in the pleasures of gianduia through chocolates, gelato, and pastries.

RISOTTO: Piedmontese cuisine reveres rice, notably through dishes like risotto. Arborio and Carnaroli rice thrive in the region's fertile plains. Treat yourself to classic saffron-infused risotto alla Milanese or panissa—a hearty rice dish enriched with beans and vegetables.

CHEESES: Piedmont crafts exceptional cheeses such as Castelmagno, Bra, and Toma. Elevate their flavors by pairing them with honey, fruit preserves, or crusty bread for a delightful culinary experience.

BAGNA CAUDA: Bagna cauda is a classic Piedmontese delicacy—a warm dip made with garlic and anchovies. Dive into the experience by dipping raw vegetables like cardoons, peppers, and artichokes into this flavorful sauce. It's a communal dish cherished during gatherings.

AGNOLOTTI DEL PLIN: These small, hand-pinched pasta pockets are stuffed with either meat or vegetables. Served with butter and sage or a rich meat sauce, each bite encapsulates the comfort and tradition of Piedmontese cuisine.

VITELLO TONNATO: A timeless appetizer showcasing thinly sliced veal topped with a creamy tuna and caper sauce. The blend of tender meat and tangy sauce provides an authentic taste of Piedmont.

Savory Piedmontese Dishes

1. *Tajarin with White Truffle from Alba*: This pasta dish features handcrafted tajarin, seasoned with butter, pepper, and freshly grated white truffle, a prized ingredient from the region. A sprinkle of Parmigiano adds an extra layer of richness. Enjoy it alongside a glass of dry red wine for a truly indulgent experience.

2. *Bagna Cauda:* A cornerstone of Piedmontese cuisine, bagna cauda, meaning "hot bath," is an olive oil-based fondue infused with anchovies and garlic. Traditionally served over an open flame to maintain warmth, it serves as the focal point of the table, complemented by other foods and wine.

3. *Mixed Fry Piedmontese Style*: This dish encompasses a variety of fried foods, including vegetables, meats, and cheese. The Piedmontese rendition often includes delicacies like zucchini flowers, sage leaves, and rabbit. Crispy and full of flavor, it's perfect for sharing.

4. *Veal with Tuna Sauce (Vitello Tonnato):* Delicate slices of veal are chilled and adorned with a creamy tuna sauce. This classic antipasto harmonizes tender meat with tangy nuances.

5. *Barolo Risotto:* Reflecting Piedmont's renowned Barolo wine, this risotto is infused with its rich essence.

Arborio rice cooked with Barolo wine results in a luxurious and fragrant dish.

6. *Gorgonzola:* Though not native to Piedmont, Gorgonzola cheese is a beloved regional favorite. With its characteristic blue or green veins, this cow's milk cheese offers a bold flavor.

7. *Panissa:* A rustic creation crafted from chickpea flour, Panissa resembles polenta. Sliced and fried to crispy perfection, it makes for delightful snacking or serves as a side dish.

8. *Mixed Boiled Meats (Bollito Misto):* This hearty dish features a medley of boiled meats like beef, veal, and chicken. Traditionally served with various flavorful sauces such as salsa verde (parsley-based) and mostarda (spicy fruit compote), Bollito Misto is a comforting communal meal enjoyed during special gatherings.

9. *Agnolotti del Plin:* These small, handmade pasta parcels are a specialty of Piedmont. Typically filled with roasted meat, vegetables, and cheese, they are delicately folded and served with butter and sage or a rich meat sauce, showcasing the region's pasta-making mastery.

10. *Braised Beef in Barolo Wine (Brasato al Barolo):* Succulent beef is slowly braised in Barolo wine, resulting in tender, flavorful meat infused with the wine's richness. Often accompanied by creamy polenta or mashed potatoes, this dish is a testament to Piedmont's culinary prowess.

11. *Bonet:* A classic Piedmontese dessert, bonet is a baked custard enriched with cocoa, amaretti cookies, and caramel. With its smooth texture and harmonious blend of flavors, it's best enjoyed chilled as a delightful finale to a satisfying meal.

12. *Piedmontese Hazelnut Cake (Torta di Nocciole):* Celebrating the region's renowned hazelnuts, this cake is moist, nutty, and bursting with flavor.

Often served with a dollop of whipped cream or a scoop of vanilla gelato, it's a perfect way to conclude a Piedmontese feast.

Indulgent Desserts and Sweets

Piedmontese desserts are a delightful blend of tradition, flavor, and local ingredients. Let's explore some of the renowned Piedmontese sweets that are sure to satisfy your sweet cravings:

Panna Cotta: A classic example of simplicity, panna cotta, meaning "cooked cream," is a silky pudding made with cream. Often accompanied by a drizzle of caramel or a berry compote, it's a must-try dessert. Sample it at Bovio in La Morra.

Gianduiotto: These iconic Piedmontese chocolates are crafted from gianduia, a velvety blend of cocoa, sugar, and roasted hazelnuts. Treat yourself to these delectable pralines at Baratti & Milano in Turin.

Baci di Dama: Translating to *"lady's kisses,"* these traditional hazelnut butter cookies feature a layer of chocolate-hazelnut spread sandwiched between them. Discover them at Pasticceria Zanotti in Tortona.

Zabaione: A luscious custard cream with a mysterious origin, zabaione is made from egg yolks, sugar, and Marsala wine. Enjoy it warm alongside ladyfingers or fresh fruit, a true Piedmontese delight.

Bonèt: Dating back to the 13th century, this indulgent dessert blends amaretti cookies (or hazelnut biscuits), eggs, cocoa powder, sugar, milk, and rum. Experience this timeless treat at L'Acino in Turin.

Torta Novecento (Chocolate Cake): Crafted to mark the beginning of the 20th century, this decadent chocolate cake features layers of rich chocolate. Indulge in it at Pasticceria Balla in Ivrea.

Krumiri: These traditional Piedmontese cookies, originating from 1870, are made with fresh eggs, flour, sugar, butter, and vanilla. Their unique twisted shape adds to their charm. Explore them in Casale Monferrato.

Gianduia Gelato: Combining the flavors of hazelnuts and milk chocolate, this gelato flavor is a beloved choice in Piedmont. Treat yourself to a scoop at Gelateria Alberto Marchetti in Turin.

Paste di Meliga: These cornmeal cookies are a delightful specialty of northern Italy. Whether sweet or savory, their crumbly texture makes them irresistible.

PIEDMONTESE TRUFFLES:

> ➢ White Truffle (Tartufo Bianco d'Alba)

The highly sought-after Tartufo Bianco d'Alba is a prized truffle variety found in Piedmont. Often referred to as "white gold" due to its rarity and exceptional flavor profile, it emits a captivating aroma. Accompanied by skilled dogs, truffle hunters venture into the wooded hills to unearth these treasures. The white truffle season lasts from October to December, filling the air with its earthy fragrance. Alba hosts the International Fair of the Alba White Truffle, a bustling market where enthusiasts gather to celebrate and purchase these culinary gems. Additionally, the Alba White Truffle World Auction, held in November, showcases the finest specimens and supports charitable causes.

> ➤ **Truffle Hunting Regulations**

Truffle hunting, deeply ingrained in Piedmontese tradition, entails navigating forests guided by trained dogs. Hunters are required to comply with regulations governing non-cultivated areas and obtain permits following successful completion of a state exam..

> ➤ **Varieties of Piedmontese Truffles**

In addition to the revered white truffle, Piedmont offers a variety of other truffle types. Among them is the Moscato Truffle, which can be found between January and March and is particularly well-suited for enhancing sauces and pâtés. Harvested in March and April, the Bianchetto Truffle is commonly found near chestnut and pine roots. Summer Truffles, also known as Scorzone, are available from May to July and offer a milder flavor. Finally, the White Truffle, known as Tartufo Bianco d'Alba, is sought after from September to December and is considered the pinnacle of truffle excellence.

PIEDMONTESE WINE:

1. Barolo: Barolo, often referred to as the "king of wines," originates from the town of Barolo and is exclusively crafted from Nebbiolo grapes. Renowned for their robustness, complexity, and aging potential, these wines captivate wine enthusiasts worldwide. Barolo vineyards provide stunning vistas of rolling hills and charming villages, offering a picturesque backdrop for wine appreciation.

2. Barbaresco: Considered as the sophisticated counterpart to Barolo, Barbaresco is another exquisite Nebbiolo-based wine. Originating from the village of Barbaresco, these wines possess a slightly softer and more approachable character, especially in their youth. Visitors have the opportunity to appreciate medieval architecture and delve into charming wine cellars while enjoying the delights of Barbaresco wines.

3. Other Wine-Tasting Destinations: In Neive, a picturesque village, visitors can enjoy intimate wine-tasting experiences along narrow streets. Monforte d'Alba, known for its chic ambiance and summer jazz festival, is home to excellent wineries. In addition to its truffles, Alba is renowned for its vibrant wine scene, inviting visitors to explore local wine shops and indulge in the finest wines Piedmont has to offer.

Where to Experience Truffle Hunting and Wine Tasting:

Embark on guided white truffle hunting tours to witness the excitement firsthand.

Learn about truffle ecology, the role of dogs, and the art of harvesting these delicacies.

Enjoy tastings of fresh truffles paired with local cheeses, salami, and Barbera D'Asti DOCG wine.

Explore charming towns such as Barolo, Barbaresco, Neive, and Monforte d'Alba.

Tour vineyards, sample wines, and immerse yourself in the rich viticultural heritage of Piedmont.

Dining and Cuisine Etiquette

The dining and cuisine etiquette observed in Piedmont reflects the region's deep-rooted culinary traditions and focus on hospitality.

Here are some important points to consider:

1. Respect for Local Ingredients: Piedmontese cuisine is renowned for its utilization of fresh, locally sourced ingredients. Show respect for the region's culinary legacy by embracing dishes crafted with seasonal fruits, vegetables, meats, and cheeses.

2. Embracing Slow Food: Piedmont is where the Slow Food movement originated, emphasizing the value of leisurely dining and relishing each mouthful. Take your time to savor the flavors and textures of traditional Piedmontese dishes.

3. Appreciating Wine Pairings: Wine plays a significant role in Piedmontese dining culture. Enhance your dining experience by pairing local wines with your meal. Explore regional varieties such as Barolo, Barbaresco, and Barbera, which complement Piedmontese cuisine beautifully.

4. Observing Table Manners: When dining in Piedmont, adhere to basic table etiquette, including keeping your elbows off the table, using utensils correctly, and waiting for everyone to be served before starting your meal. It's customary to say "Buon appetito" or "Enjoy your meal" before beginning.

5. Expressing Gratitude: Show appreciation to your hosts or restaurant staff for their hospitality and the delicious meal provided. A simple "Grazie" (thank you) goes a long way in expressing gratitude for the dining experience.

6. Tipping Etiquette: While tipping is not obligatory in Italy, as a service charge is often included in the bill,

leaving a small tip is customary for exceptional service. This gesture serves as a token of appreciation.

By embracing these dining and cuisine etiquette guidelines, you'll not only relish the flavors of Piedmont but also immerse yourself in its vibrant culinary heritage.

IMMERSING IN PIEDMONT CULTURE

Art and Architecture

1. Royal Residences: Piedmont boasts the Royal Residences of the House of Savoy, recognized as a UNESCO World Heritage Site. These lavish palaces and churches exhibit exquisite Baroque design. Noteworthy examples include the Royal Palace in Turin, the Royal Church of San Lorenzo, and the Chapel of the Holy Shroud, all graced with the elegant touch of architect Guarino Guarini.

2. Palazzo Carignano: Designed by Guarini in the late 17th century, Palazzo Carignano stands as a majestic architectural marvel. Its graceful facade and intricate brickwork epitomize Italian Baroque art, enhanced by its rich historical significance.

3. Superga Basilica: Situated atop a hill overlooking the Po River, the Superga Basilica seamlessly blends Baroque and neoclassical styles.

Its architectural beauty, coupled with sweeping panoramic views, makes it an essential destination for visitors.

4. Chapel of Sant'Uberto: Found outside Turin, this chapel, crafted by architect Filippo Juvarra, reflects the grandeur of court life at the Reggia di Venaria. Its balanced proportions and detailed ornamentation stand as a testament to Juvarra's architectural prowess.

5. Palazzina di Caccia di Stupinigi: Conceived by Juvarra, the Hunting Lodge of Stupinigi is a masterpiece of European architecture. Its grand interiors, lavish furnishings, and impeccable craftsmanship showcase the pinnacle of Piedmontese Baroque design.

6. Sacri Monti (Sacred Mounts): These UNESCO World Heritage Sites seamlessly blend art, spirituality, and natural beauty. From Varallo in Valsesia to Oropa in the Pre-Alps of Biella, these mountaintop complexes feature ornate chapels, sculptures, and breathtaking vistas.

Explore the refined churches and stately palaces in historic towns like Asti. In Casale Monferrato, uncover the remarkable baroque synagogue constructed in 1595—an enduring symbol of Piedmont's diverse cultural heritage.

Music and Festivals

The Monforte D'Alba Jazz Festival (July to August) celebrates its 40th anniversary, drawing music enthusiasts worldwide. Esteemed jazz artists like Paolo Conte and Ute Lemper grace the stage, enchanting audiences amidst the scenic backdrop of Monforte d'Alba. Attendees can savor exceptional performances while indulging in the delectable offerings of Piedmontese cuisine.

The Palio of Asti (1 September), Italy's oldest Palio, unfolds in Asti every first Sunday of September, steeped in nearly a millennium of tradition. Experience the exhilarating horse race and immerse yourself in the festive ambiance.

September in Piedmont also hosts additional events such as the Festival Delle Sagre and the Douja D'Or wine festival.

Asti's Festival of Festivals (7-8 September) transforms into Europe's largest open-air restaurant, inviting visitors to sample a diverse range of food and wine offerings amidst the bustling streets of Asti.

Other Cultural Events:

The Historical Parade of Palio (1 September) leads up to the horse race, featuring a series of events where each district and suburb showcases representative objects. Participants also organize propitiatory dinners before the Historical Horse Race.

Sacri Monti (Sacred Mounts), recognized as UNESCO World Heritage Sites, blend art, spirituality, and nature. Explore sites like Varallo in Valsesia and Oropa in the Pre-Alps of Biella.

Piedmont hosts various food and wine festivals, art exhibitions, and historical re-enactments. From the Palio of Asti to the Cioccolatò festival and Wine Street tasting, there's always something exciting happening in the region.

Local Traditions and Customs

1. Annual Festivals and Events: Piedmont hosts a plethora of festivals and events that honor its rich traditions and historical significance. Occasions like the Alba White Truffle Fair, the Palio di Asti horse race, and the renowned Battle of the Oranges in Ivrea are beloved traditions that attract both locals and tourists alike.

2. Gastronomic Culture: Piedmontese cuisine is renowned for its robust flavors and utilization of locally sourced ingredients. From the prized truffles and hazelnuts to the distinguished Barolo and Barbaresco wines, food and wine play pivotal roles in social gatherings and festivities.

Family gatherings often feature communal meals accompanied by animated conversations.

3. Craftsmanship: Piedmont boasts a storied tradition of artisanal craftsmanship, encompassing a wide array of disciplines such as textiles, ceramics, woodworking, and glassblowing. Exploring local markets and workshops offers insight into the mastery and ingenuity of these artisans, offering visitors the opportunity to acquire unique handmade treasures.

4. Religious Observances: Piedmont's cultural fabric is woven with strong religious ties, evident in the myriad of religious processions, festivals, and ceremonies held throughout the year. These events often incorporate traditional rituals, music, and elaborate displays of religious iconography, showcasing the region's deep-rooted spiritual heritage.

5. *Language and Dialects:* While Italian serves as the official language of Piedmont, the region boasts its own distinct dialects and linguistic traditions. Familiarizing oneself with a few phrases in the local dialect can foster a deeper connection with residents and enhance the overall experience of exploration.

6. *Outdoor Pursuits:* The diverse landscape of Piedmont, spanning from the majestic Alps to the picturesque hills of Langhe and Monferrato, offers abundant opportunities for outdoor recreation. Activities such as hiking, skiing, cycling, and wine tasting tours are popular among both locals and visitors, providing immersive experiences within the region's natural splendor.

7. *Community Engagement:* Community events and gatherings, including village fairs, markets, and traditional music festivals, form integral components of Piedmontese culture.

These gatherings serve as occasions for community members to unite, celebrate shared heritage, and reinforce social bonds, embodying the region's warmth and hospitality.

Exploring these local customs and traditions affords visitors a deeper appreciation of Piedmont's cultural legacy and the chance to immerse themselves in its distinctive allure and hospitality.

Museums and Galleries

✓ Egyptian Museum (Museo Egizio)

Situated in Turin, the Egyptian Museum boasts an extensive assortment of Egyptian relics.

Visitors can explore ancient mummies, sculptures, and hieroglyphic inscriptions.

It stands as one of the most comprehensive collections of Egyptian artifacts outside of Egypt.

- ✓ National Cinema Museum (Museo Nazionale del Cinema)

Nestled within Turin's iconic Mole Antonelliana, this museum celebrates the artistry of cinema.

Guests can delve into the history of film, view iconic movie props, and enjoy interactive displays.

Don't forget to experience the breathtaking panoramic view from the top of the Mole.

- ✓ National Automobile Museum (Museo Nazionale dell'Automobile)

Located in Turin, this museum is a haven for automobile enthusiasts.

Visitors can explore vintage cars, delve into Formula 1 history, and admire automotive-themed art installations.

It offers a fascinating journey through the evolution of automobiles.

✓ Borromeo Palace (Palazzo Borromeo)

This historic palace in Turin showcases art galleries, picturesque grottos, and meticulously manicured gardens.

Guests can marvel at exquisite artwork while enjoying the tranquil ambiance of the surroundings.

✓ Royal Armory (Armeria Reale)

Positioned in Turin, the Royal Armory exhibits an impressive array of weaponry and armor.

Guests can delve into the history of military warfare while exploring the collection of historical arms and armor.

ART GALLERIES:

1. *Sabauda Gallery (Galleria Sabauda):* Located within Turin's Royal Palace, the Sabauda Gallery houses a remarkable assemblage of art pieces, where guests can admire works by renowned Italian and European artists,

including paintings from the Renaissance and Baroque periods.

2. Giovanni and Marella Agnelli Gallery (Pinacoteca Giovanni e Marella Agnelli): Situated in Turin, this gallery showcases contemporary art and design, offering visitors a diverse collection of paintings, sculptures, and modern artworks to enjoy..

3. Civic Museum of Ancient Art (Museo Civico d'Arte Antica): Located in Turin, this museum offers a glimpse into the region's rich artistic heritage through ancient art and artifacts.

4. Museum of Oriental Art (Turin): Guests can immerse themselves in Asian art and culture through traditional paintings, ceramics, and sculptures housed in this museum.

5. Stupinigi Hunting Lodge (Palazzina di Caccia of Stupinigi): This Baroque masterpiece, situated near Turin, showcases grand halls, lavish interiors, and stunning gardens, offering visitors a glimpse into aristocratic life.

Public holidays

1. New Year's Day (Capodanno) - January 1st: This holiday marks the start of the new year and is celebrated with various festivities, parties, and firework displays.

2. Epiphany (Epifania) - January 6th: Epiphany commemorates the visit of the Magi to the infant Jesus and is observed with traditional customs, including the arrival of La Befana, a folklore figure who brings gifts to children.

3. Easter Monday (Pasquetta) - Date varies (usually in March or April): This day, known as "Little Easter," follows Easter Sunday and is a time for leisure activities and gatherings with loved ones.

4. Liberation Day (Festa della Liberazione) - April 25th: Liberation Day honors the end of Nazi occupation in Italy during World War II and is marked with national ceremonies, parades, and patriotic events.

5. Labor Day (Festa del Lavoro) - May 1st: Labor Day celebrates the achievements of workers and the labor movement with demonstrations, rallies, and cultural activities organized by labor unions.

6. Republic Day (Festa della Repubblica) - June 2nd: Republic Day commemorates the establishment of the Italian Republic and is observed with official ceremonies, flag-raising ceremonies, and cultural festivities.

7. Feast of the Assumption (Ferragosto) - August 15th: Ferragosto celebrates the Catholic feast of the Assumption of Mary and is a traditional time for vacations, outdoor activities, and gatherings with family and friends.

8. All Saints' Day (Ognissanti) - November 1st: All Saints' Day honors all saints and martyrs recognized the Catholic Church and is observed with visits to cemeteries, religious services, and remembrance of deceased loved ones.

9. Feast of the Immaculate Conception (Immacolata Concezione) - December 8th: This holiday celebrates the belief in the Virgin Mary's conception without original sin and is marked by religious observances, including Masses and processions.

10. Christmas Day (Natale) - December 25th: Christmas Day commemorates the birth of Jesus Christ and is celebrated with religious services, gift-giving, and festive meals shared with family and friends.

11. St. Stephen's Day (Santo Stefano) - December 26th: St. Stephen's Day honors the first Christian martyr and is a time for relaxation, visiting relatives, and enjoying leftover Christmas feasts.

Language and piedmont mini dictionary

Piedmontese (also known as piemontèis or lenga piemontèisa) is a language spoken by roughly 2 million individuals, primarily in the Piedmont region of Northwest Italy.

Despite being recognized as a distinct language by linguists, it is often mistakenly considered an Italian dialect. Here are some key aspects of Piedmontese:

Linguistic Group: It falls within the Gallo-Italic languages group of Northern Italy, alongside Lombard, Emilian, Ligurian, and Romagnolo.

Geographic Distribution: Piedmontese is predominantly spoken in Piedmont, with additional pockets in northwestern Liguria (near Savona) and select municipalities in Lombardy (specifically western Lomellina near Pavia).

Literary Heritage: The earliest known Piedmontese documents date back to the 12th century, referred to as the sermones subalpini. Notable poets like Zan Zòrs Alion contributed secular literary works during the Renaissance.

Endangered Status: Classified as "Definitely Endangered" by the UNESCO Atlas of the World's Languages in Danger in 2010, Piedmontese faces challenges to its preservation and usage.

Diaspora: Migration from Italy has led to the spread of Piedmontese to regions such as the Argentinian Pampas, where many Piedmontese immigrants settled.

Brazil: Piedmontese is also spoken in certain states of Brazil, alongside the Venetian language.

MINI DICTIONARY

Adiù | Hello

A warm greeting to initiate conversations.

Ciào

Equivalent to the Italian 'ciao' (informal).

Use it interchangeably for both "hello" and "goodbye."

Grassie / Mersì | Thanks

Convey appreciation with these expressions.

Nen / Pa | No

Helpful for basic interactions.

Arvëdse/ Arvèisse | Goodbye

Bid adieu in Piedmontese.

Bun di | Good morning

A pleasant morning greeting.

Buon dì | Good day

  Use it throughout the day as a friendly salutation.

Piacere | Nice to meet you

Express your pleasure upon meeting someone new.

Dov'è il bagno? | Where is the bathroom?

A crucial inquiry for travelers!

Quanto costa? | How much does it cost?

Useful for shopping or dining inquiries.

Posso avere il conto? | Can I have the bill?

When you're ready to settle the bill at a restaurant.

Mi scusi | Excuse me

Politely get someone's attention.

Per favore | Please

Always add politeness to your requests.

Mi chiamo.. | My name is...

Introduce yourself in Piedmontese.

Dove si trova...?| Where is...?

Ask for directions to a specific location.

Mi piace molto | I like it a lot

Express your fondness for something.

Buon viaggio | Have a good trip

Wish fellow travelers well.

Buon appetito | Enjoy your meal

Say this before beginning a meal.

Mi dispiace | I'm sorry

Offer apologies when necessary.

Che bello! | How beautiful!

Show admiration for something stunning.

Che buono! | How delicious!

Express enjoyment of tasty food.

Sì | Yes

Keep responses straightforward.

No | No

Use for simple negative responses.

Grazie mille | Thank you very much

Show extra gratitude.

Arrivederci | Goodbye

Bid farewell to new acquaintances.

MUST-VISIT ATTRACTIONS IN PIEDMONT

Royal Residences and Palaces

Royal Palace of Turin (Palazzo Reale di Torino)

The Royal Palace of Turin stands as a symbol of the House of Savoy's wealth and grandeur. Initially constructed in the 16th century, it underwent significant renovations during the 17th century under Christine Marie of France. Alongside the main building, the palace complex includes the Palazzo Chiablese and the Chapel of the Holy Shroud, built specifically to house the renowned Shroud of Turin, believed by some to be the burial cloth of Jesus Christ.

Architect Filippo Juvarra contributed Baroque elements to the palace's design, notably seen in the splendid **Hall of Diana, a masterpiece adorned with intricate details. Surrounding the palace, extensive grounds and gardens feature archaeological remnants and 17th-century grottos, complemented by contemporary sculptures.

Hosting a vibrant events program, the Royal Palace hosts concerts and educational workshops.

Reggia di Venaria (La Venaria Reale)

Often dubbed "Turin's Versailles," the Reggia di Venaria is an impressive Baroque estate. Commissioned in the 17th century by Duke Carlo Emanuele II of Savoy, it spans a remarkable 80,000 square meters, comprising vast grounds, gardens, and archaeological sites. A highlight is the Hall of Diana, designed by Amedeo di Castellamonte, a stunning example of Baroque architecture. La Venaria Reale hosts numerous exhibitions, cultural events, and guided tours, inviting visitors to explore its lavish interiors and meticulously landscaped gardens.

Palazzo Madama

Nestled in the heart of Turin, Palazzo Madama boasts a rich history. Originally a Roman gate, it evolved into a medieval castle before serving as the residence of the Madama Reale (Queen Mother).

The palace showcases a blend of architectural styles, including Roman, medieval, and Baroque, evident in its elegant façade adorned with balconies and sculptures. Inside, visitors can admire its grand halls, galleries, and the magnificent spiral staircase designed by Filippo Juvarra. Housing the Museum of Ancient Art, Palazzo Madama hosts an impressive collection of paintings, sculptures, and decorative arts.

Palazzo Carignano

Another architectural marvel in Turin, Palazzo Carignano is a Baroque masterpiece crafted by Guarino Guarini. Notable for its undulating façade, intricate stonework, and elliptical courtyard, the palace holds historical significance as the birthplace of Victor Emmanuel II, the first King of Italy. Today, it houses the Museum of the Risorgimento, dedicated to Italy's unification history. Visitors can explore exhibits featuring artifacts, documents, and paintings from this transformative period.

Palazzina di Caccia of Stupinigi

Situated on the outskirts of Turin, the Hunting Lodge of Stupinigi is a captivating Baroque retreat designed by Filippo Juvarra for the Savoy family. Featuring grand halls, lavish interiors, and meticulously landscaped gardens, the lodge served as a hunting sanctuary. Its central oval hall, adorned with frescoes and stucco work, stands out as a focal point. The expansive parkland surrounding Stupinigi invites leisurely exploration and scenic strolls.

Historic Castles and Fortresses

Royal Palace of Turin (Palazzo Reale di Torino): The Royal Palace of Turin stands as a symbol of the opulence and grandeur of the House of Savoy. Constructed initially in the 16th century, it underwent substantial renovations under Christine Marie of France in the 17th century.

Alongside the main building, the palace complex includes the Palazzo Chiablese and the Chapel of the Holy Shroud, specifically built to house the renowned Shroud of Turin. Architect Filippo Juvarra infused Baroque elements into the palace's design, evident in the splendid Hall of Diana he designed. Surrounding the palace, extensive grounds and gardens feature archaeological remnants, 17th-century grottos, and contemporary sculptures, creating a harmonious blend of history and art. The Royal Palace hosts a vibrant events program, offering concerts and educational workshops.

Reggia di Venaria (La Venaria Reale): Often dubbed "Turin's Versailles," the Reggia di Venaria is a majestic Baroque estate commissioned in the 17th century by Duke Carlo Emanuele II of Savoy. Spanning an impressive 80,000 square meters, the estate encompasses vast grounds, gardens, and archaeological sites.

A standout feature is the Hall of Diana, a masterpiece of Baroque architecture designed by Amedeo di Castellamonte. La Venaria Reale welcomes visitors with various exhibitions, cultural events, and guided tours, inviting them to explore its lavish interiors and meticulously landscaped gardens.

Palazzo Madama: Situated in the heart of Turin, Palazzo Madama boasts a rich history, evolving from a Roman gate to a medieval castle before becoming the residence of the Madama Reale (Queen Mother). The palace showcases a fusion of architectural styles, including Roman, medieval, and Baroque, evident in its captivating façade adorned with balconies and sculptures.

Inside, visitors can marvel at the grand halls, galleries, and the magnificent spiral staircase designed by Filippo Juvarra. Housing the Museum of Ancient Art, Palazzo Madama offers a fascinating journey through its impressive collection of paintings, sculptures, and decorative arts.

Palazzo Carignano

Another architectural gem in Turin, Palazzo Carignano is a Baroque masterpiece crafted by Guarino Guarini. Distinguished by its undulating façade, intricate stonework, and elliptical courtyard, the palace holds historical significance as the birthplace of Victor Emmanuel II, the first King of Italy. Today, it is home to the Museum of the Risorgimento, dedicated to the history of Italian unification. Visitors can delve into the museum's exhibits, which include artifacts, documents, and paintings related to this transformative period in Italy's past.

Palazzina di Caccia of Stupinigi

Nestled just outside Turin, the Hunting Lodge of Stupinigi is a splendid Baroque retreat designed by Filippo Juvarra for the Savoy family. Featuring grand halls, sumptuous interiors, and meticulously landscaped gardens, the lodge served as a serene hunting sanctuary.

Its central oval hall, adorned with frescoes and stucco work, serves as a highlight of the visit. The expansive parkland surrounding Stupinigi invites visitors to immerse themselves in its natural beauty and enjoy leisurely strolls amidst history and tranquility.

CHARMING VILLAGES AND TOWNS

Orta San Giulio:

Dubbed "God's watercolor," this charming village nestled on Lake Orta is a well-kept secret.

Wander through its quaint cobblestone streets, marvel at the pastel-hued buildings, and soak in the serene lake vistas.

Embark on a boat excursion to the tiny Isola San Giulio, a tranquil island sanctuary.

Stresa

Situated on Lake Maggiore, Stresa exudes a refined resort ambiance.

Explore the enchanting Borromean Islands via ferry, each offering its own distinct allure.

The iconic Grand Hotel, where Hemingway found inspiration for "A Farewell to Arms," adds a touch of allure.

Barolo

Renowned for its fine wines, Barolo is a must-visit destination in the Langhe region.

Meander through its peaceful streets, indulge in local gastronomic delights, and wander amid the surrounding vineyards.

The panoramic Langhe hills provide a breathtaking backdrop to this picturesque town.

Neive

Perched atop a hill, Neive is a medieval gem boasting well-preserved architecture, including ancient towers and stone dwellings.

Delight in wine tastings at nearby vineyards and relish the unhurried pace of life.

Ricetto di Candelo

This medieval hamlet near Biella serves as a living testament to history.

Encircled by ancient fortifications, it features charming stone houses, arched passageways, and inviting courtyards.

Explore artisan workshops and immerse yourself in the ambiance of yesteryears.

Vogogna:

Vogogna's cobblestone streets lead to a fairytale-like castle overlooking the village.

Admire the fresco-adorned halls of the Visconti Castle and bask in the tranquility of alpine vistas.

Bra

Bra beckons food enthusiasts with its culinary delights.

Visit the renowned Slow Food headquarters and meander through the historic town center.

The annual Cheese Festival is a highlight, attracting cheese aficionados from far and wide.

Saluzzo

Saluzzo charms visitors with its medieval ambiance and impeccably preserved historic core.

Explore landmarks such as the Palazzo Comunale, the Cathedral, and the picturesque Piazza Castello.

Venture into the surrounding hills for scenic hikes and panoramic views.

Cherasco

Cherasco's elegant arcades and charming squares exude timeless allure.

Discover architectural gems like the Church of San Pietro and delve into local history at the Civic Museum.

Don't miss the annual Snail Festival, a celebration of the region's culinary heritage.

Cuneo

Vibrant Cuneo is embraced by the majestic Alps.

Explore the bustling Piazza Galimberti and admire the 12th-century Cathedral.

Outdoor enthusiasts will delight in the year-round adventures offered by the nearby Maritime Alps.

Hidden Gems Off the Beaten Path

Venturing off the well-trodden paths in Piedmont reveals hidden treasures often missed by tourists. Here are some lesser-known gems waiting to be explored:

1. Sanctuary of Saint Michael (Santuario di San Michele): Nestled on Mount Pirchiriano near Turin, this ancient abbey boasts breathtaking panoramic views of the Susa Valley. Its medieval architecture and tranquil atmosphere provide a serene escape for those seeking peace and spirituality.

2. Ricetto di Candelo: Situated near Biella, this medieval fortified village is a perfectly preserved gem surrounded by ancient walls and towers. Walking through its narrow streets feels like stepping back in time, offering a glimpse into Piedmont's rich history.

3. Sacred Mountain of Varallo (Sacro Monte di Varallo): Recognized as a UNESCO World Heritage Site, this sacred mountain in Valsesia is adorned with chapels and religious sculptures dating back to the 16th century.

Its intricate artworks and serene ambiance create a hidden sanctuary for art and spirituality.

4. Nivolet Pass (Colle del Nivolet): Nature enthusiasts will delight in this remote mountain pass within Gran Paradiso National Park. Serpentine roads lead to breathtaking vistas, alpine lakes, and hiking trails, offering a tranquil escape from the hustle and bustle.

5. Zegna Oasis (Oasi Zegna): Nestled in the Biellese Alps, this nature reserve is a haven for outdoor enthusiasts and wildlife admirers. Serene walking paths wind through lush forests, meadows, and pastures, providing opportunities for birdwatching and picnicking amidst nature's beauty.

6. Roero Rocks (Rocche del Roero): These ancient rock formations near Alba are a marvel of nature, shaped by centuries of erosion. Hiking trails lead to panoramic viewpoints overlooking the Tanaro River valley, offering a unique perspective of Piedmont's rugged terrain.

7. Pralormo Castle (Castello di Pralormo): Situated in the Asti province, this enchanting castle is surrounded by expansive gardens and whimsical topiary sculptures. Visitors can meander through labyrinthine paths, discover hidden grottos, and admire vibrant floral displays, creating a fairytale-like experience.

Exploring these hidden gems off the beaten path allows you to uncover Piedmont's lesser-known treasures and immerse yourself in the region's diverse landscapes, history, and culture in a unique and authentic manner.

OUTDOOR ADVENTURES

Hiking and Trekking Trails

1. Barolo - La Morra via Castello della Volta: You can enjoy a leisurely walk through cultivated fields, ancient castles, and charming towns. This route connects Barolo and La Morra, mainly following accessible dirt roads. Along the way, take in scenic vineyard views and explore the delightful villages that line the path.

2. Lake Mergozzo Loop: You can embark on a scenic trek along the southern shore of Lake Mergozzo, following the blue trail. Although the trail features rocky and challenging stretches, hikers are treated to breathtaking views of both Lake Mergozzo and Lake Maggiore as their reward.

3. Turin City Center: Explore Turin's landmarks by foot, visiting iconic monuments, squares, pedestrian zones, and parks. Experience the city's Roman grid layout and marvel at its Baroque architecture.

4. Alpeggi sopra Cicogna - Giro ad anello: Embark on a circular trail around Alpeggi sopra Cicogna, where you can revel in panoramic mountain vistas and immerse yourself in the natural surroundings.

5. From Devero to Vannino: A 2-day trek: Embark on a challenging two-day trek from Devero to Vannino, traversing rugged terrain and witnessing the beauty of the Alps firsthand.

Skiing and Snowboarding Destinations

Among Piedmont's standout ski areas is the Milky Way (Via Lattea), renowned for its expansive terrain that extends into France. This region encompasses top-notch resorts like Sestriere, Sauze d'Oulx, and Claviere, offering a wide range of slopes suitable for beginners to expert-level skiers and snowboarders.

Another popular spot is Bardonecchia, which hosted snowboarding events during the 2006 Winter Olympics. With its vast ski area and modern amenities, Bardonecchia attracts thrill-seekers looking for challenging runs and exciting terrain parks.

For those yearning for a more traditional alpine experience, Limone Piemonte provides a charming mix of stunning scenery and historical allure. Nestled in the Maritime Alps, Limone Piemonte boasts scenic tree-lined slopes and a quaint village atmosphere, appealing to families and leisure skiers alike.

In addition to these well-known resorts, Piedmont offers a variety of smaller ski areas and hidden gems such as Prato Nevoso, Alagna Valsesia, and Pian della Regina. These lesser-known destinations offer a more intimate and authentic alpine experience, with quieter slopes and a friendly ambiance.

Whether you're an experienced snow enthusiast or hitting the slopes for the first time, Piedmont's ski resorts offer unforgettable winter adventures. From thrilling downhill descents to leisurely explorations of snow-covered landscapes, Piedmont promises something special for every visitor amidst its snowy mountain vistas.

Cycling Routes and Bike Tours

The Langhe region stands out as a favored destination for cyclists, renowned for its vineyards and enchanting hilltop settlements. Cyclists can traverse routes winding through vineyard-clad hills, pausing to taste acclaimed wines and savor local cuisine along the journey.

Similarly, the Monferrato area boasts excellent cycling opportunities, characterized by its gentle hills and medieval villages. Cyclists can pedal through scenic countryside, passing by historic castles, ancient churches, and quaint rural communities.

For those seeking more challenging terrain, the alpine landscapes of the Western Alps provide exhilarating cycling routes offering awe-inspiring mountain vistas. Cyclists can conquer mountain passes like the Colle delle Finestre and the Colle del Nivolet, both of which have been featured in prestigious cycling races such as the Giro d'Italia.

Piedmont also hosts several long-distance cycling paths, including the renowned Ciclovia Alpe Adria, linking Salzburg in Austria to Grado on the Adriatic Sea. Cyclists can journey through picturesque landscapes encompassing mountain ranges, rivers, and cultural landmarks on this remarkable cycling odyssey.

Moreover, bike tours and guided cycling experiences abound throughout Piedmont, providing cyclists with opportunities to discover the region's highlights alongside knowledgeable local guides.

These tours often include visits to wineries, historical sites, and scenic viewpoints, offering participants a comprehensive and immersive cycling encounter.

Whether you're a casual cyclist seeking to enjoy the countryside or a seasoned rider in search of challenging ascents, Piedmont offers a plethora of cycling routes and tours tailored to every preference and skill level.

Adventure Sports and Activities

Hiking and Trekking: Embark on scenic trails in the Langhe region, where vineyards seamlessly merge with rolling hills. Venture into the Gran Paradiso National Park, an ideal setting for hiking, camping, and fishing. Experience the breathtaking views along the Lake Mergozzo Loop.

Skiing and Snowboarding: Given its proximity to the French and Swiss Alps, Piedmont is a top destination for winter sports enthusiasts.

Experience exhilarating descents at resorts like Prato Nevoso or explore the Turin Alps for even more adventure.

Mountain Biking and Cycling: Cycle through charming villages, vineyards, and scenic countryside landscapes. Explore the Barolo-La Morra route, known for its vineyard vistas and historical landmarks.

Rafting and Canyoning: Seek excitement in Valsesia with adrenaline-pumping rafting, kayaking, and canyoning adventures on the Sesia River. Consider Monrosa Rafting for a thrilling escapade.

Paragliding and Hot Air Ballooning: Take flight above the Alps with thrilling paragliding experiences. Drift through the skies on a hot air balloon for unparalleled views of the landscape.

Rock Climbing and Via Ferrata: Conquer rugged cliffs in the Alps or challenge yourself on via ferrata routes. Discover the challenging climbs and stunning vistas in the Valsesia area.

Gran Paradiso Wildlife Safari: Embark on guided wildlife safaris in the Gran Paradiso National Park. Keep an eye out for ibex, chamois, and other magnificent alpine creatures.

PRACTICAL TIPS FOR TRAVELERS

Accommodation Options; Alberghi Diffusi ,Mountain Refuges,hotels

HOTELS

1. Grand Hotel Sitea (Turin): This opulent establishment situated in the heart of Turin boasts refined accommodations, exquisite dining options, and top-notch service.

2. Villa Crespi (Orta San Giulio): Overlooking the picturesque Lake Orta, Villa Crespi captivates with its Moorish-inspired architecture, sumptuous rooms, a renowned Michelin-starred restaurant, and enchanting gardens.

3. Relais San Maurizio (Langhe): Nestled within a converted 17th-century monastery in the Langhe wine region, this boutique hotel offers luxurious lodgings, a rejuvenating spa, and epicurean delights.

4. Castello di Guarene (Guarene): Resting amid vineyard-draped hills, this meticulously restored castle beckons with its elegant rooms, wellness facilities, and sweeping vistas of Piedmont's countryside.

5. Hotel Palazzo del Carretto (Mondovì): Seamlessly blending modern comforts with medieval allure, this boutique hotel, located in Mondovì's historic quarter, features stylish rooms and a charming rooftop terrace.

6. Palazzo Righini (Fossano): Housed within an impeccably refurbished 18th-century palace, this boutique gem offers luxurious accommodations, a gastronomic haven, and a tranquil spa experience.

7. Hotel Villa Beccaris (Monforte d'Alba): Set within a historic villa overlooking the famed Barolo vineyards, this hotel invites guests to indulge in elegant rooms, a panoramic terrace, and a refreshing swimming pool.

AGRITURISMI (FARM STAYS)

Agriturismo Il Cascinale (Langhe): Located amidst the rolling hills of the Langhe wine region, Agriturismo Il Cascinale offers guests a peaceful retreat surrounded by vineyards and hazelnut orchards. Visitors can experience farm life firsthand by participating in activities such as harvesting grapes or picking fresh produce from the garden. The agriturismo also features comfortable accommodations in traditional farmhouse-style rooms and serves delicious meals made with locally sourced ingredients.

Azienda Agricola Ca' Brusà (Roero): Situated in the picturesque Roero area, Azienda Agricola Ca' Brusà invites guests to relax in a tranquil rural setting while enjoying views of the vineyards and hills. This family-run farm produces wine, hazelnuts, and other agricultural products, and visitors can learn about the cultivation process through guided tours and tastings.

Accommodations include cozy rooms with rustic charm, and guests can savor traditional Piedmontese cuisine prepared with fresh, seasonal ingredients.

Agriturismo Cascina la Barona (Monferrato): Nestled in the scenic countryside of Monferrato, Agriturismo Cascina la Barona offers a genuine farm experience combined with warm hospitality. The agriturismo features comfortable guest rooms in a renovated farmhouse, surrounded by vineyards and orchards. Guests can explore the grounds, interact with farm animals, and even join in activities like cheese making or wine tasting. The on-site restaurant serves authentic Piedmontese dishes made with organic ingredients sourced from the farm.

Agriturismo La Biandrina (Cuneo Province): Set in the stunning landscape of the Cuneo Province, Agriturismo La Biandrina provides a peaceful retreat for nature lovers and food enthusiasts alike.

The farm specializes in organic agriculture and offers guests the opportunity to tour the fields and orchards while learning about sustainable farming practices. Accommodations range from cozy rooms to self-catering apartments, and guests can enjoy homemade meals prepared with fresh ingredients sourced directly from the farm. Additionally, La Biandrina organizes outdoor activities such as hiking, cycling, and horseback riding, allowing guests to fully immerse themselves in Piedmont's natural beauty.

BED AND BREAKFASTS (B&B)

B&B Villa Cardellino (Alba): Situated in the heart of the Langhe wine region, B&B Villa Cardellino offers guests a cozy and intimate retreat surrounded by vineyards and rolling hills. The charming villa features comfortable guest rooms decorated in a rustic style, each with its own unique character.

Guests can start their day with a delicious homemade breakfast served in the picturesque garden, and the friendly hosts are happy to provide recommendations for exploring the nearby wineries, historic towns, and culinary delights of the region.

B&B Il Mulino del Tempo Perduto (Asti): Located in the historic center of Asti, B&B Il Mulino del Tempo Perduto occupies a beautifully restored 18th-century mill, offering guests a blend of old-world charm and modern comfort. The B&B features elegantly appointed rooms with antique furnishings and scenic views of the surrounding countryside. Guests can relax in the peaceful garden or enjoy a leisurely stroll to explore Asti's medieval streets, vibrant markets, and renowned wine bars. A delicious breakfast, featuring homemade pastries and local specialties, is served each morning, providing the perfect start to a day of exploration.

B&B La Terrazza sul Monferrato (Monferrato): **Perched** on a hilltop overlooking the picturesque Monferrato countryside, B&B La Terrazza sul Monferrato offers guests a tranquil escape surrounded by vineyards and orchards. The charming guesthouse features cozy rooms decorated in a rustic style, each with its own private terrace offering stunning panoramic views. Guests can relax in the lush garden, take a dip in the refreshing swimming pool, or explore the nearby medieval villages and historic landmarks. A hearty breakfast, featuring fresh local produce and homemade treats, is served on the terrace each morning, allowing guests to savor the beauty of the surrounding landscape while starting their day off right.

HOLIDAY RENTALS

1. Villa Benedetta (Lake Maggiore): Located on the shores of Lake Maggiore, Villa Benedetta offers a luxurious holiday rental experience with stunning lake views and modern amenities.

The villa features spacious living areas, multiple bedrooms, a fully equipped kitchen, and private outdoor spaces including a terrace and garden. Guests can enjoy swimming in the lake, exploring nearby attractions such as the Borromean Islands, or simply relaxing in the tranquility of *the villa's surroundings.*

Cascina San Martino (Barolo): Nestled among the vineyards of the Barolo wine region, Cascina San Martino is a beautifully restored farmhouse offering holiday rentals perfect for wine enthusiasts and nature lovers. The property features comfortable apartments with traditional Piedmontese decor, along with shared amenities such as a swimming pool, barbecue area, and panoramic terrace. Guests can explore the surrounding vineyards, sample local wines at nearby wineries, or take scenic walks through the picturesque countryside.

Apartment La Piazza (Turin): Situated in the historic center of Turin, Apartment La Piazza is a stylish holiday rental ideal for exploring the city's cultural attractions, shopping districts, and culinary scene. The apartment offers modern furnishings, a fully equipped kitchen, and convenient access to public transportation. Guests can visit landmarks such as the Mole Antonelliana, the Royal Palace of Turin, and the Egyptian Museum, or simply wander through the charming streets of the city center, stopping at cafes, restaurants, and boutiques along the way.

ALBERGHI DIFFUSI

1. Albergo Diffuso Antica Dimora San Giorgio(Viverone): Positioned in the charming village of Viverone, overlooking Lake Viverone, this albergo diffuso offers guests the opportunity to stay in meticulously restored rooms scattered across the historic center. Each room combines traditional allure with modern amenities.

The reception, restaurant, and communal spaces are distributed among various buildings, fostering an immersive experience in local culture with personalized service.

Albergo Diffuso Mosaic (Cesana Torinese): Nestled in the picturesque mountain village of Cesana Torinese, Albergo Diffuso Mosaic provides guests with a distinct lodging experience amidst the breathtaking landscapes of the Italian Alps. Accommodation options include apartments and rooms dispersed throughout the village, each adorned in a rustic Alpine style. This albergo diffuso offers convenient access to skiing, hiking, and other outdoor pursuits, as well as local establishments and cultural attractions.

Albergo Diffuso Locanda della Distilleria (Serralunga d'Alba): Tucked away in the heart of the Langhe wine region, Albergo Diffuso Locanda della Distilleria allows guests to reside in historic edifices scattered throughout the medieval village of Serralunga d'Alba.

From cozy rooms to spacious apartments, each lodging boasts traditional Piedmontese architecture alongside contemporary comforts. Visitors can explore the village's cobblestone streets, visit nearby wineries, and indulge in the region's renowned cuisine, all while experiencing the distinctive and authentic charm of an albergo diffuso.

MOUNTAIN REFUGES

1. *Guide del Cervino Refuge:*

Situated amidst the Alps in the Aosta Valley, Italy.

Offers a warm and welcoming sanctuary for mountaineers and hikers.

2. *Mountain Hut on the Alta Via dei Monti Liguri:*

Located in the village of Passo del Rastrello, at an elevation of 1050 meters above sea level.

Provides recreational amenities such as a soccer field, tennis court, bowling alley, ping-pong tables, and a children's playground.

The hut comprises a cozy living room with a fireplace, a well-equipped kitchen, a double bedroom with an extra sofa bed and a terrace, and a second bedroom with two single bunk beds and a bathroom with a shower.

Positioned in Passo del Rastrello village, at an altitude of 1050 meters.

3. Piedmont National Wildlife Refuge (PWR):

Located in central Georgia, USA.

Predominantly characterized by upland forest, with loblolly pine dominating the ridges and hardwoods lining creek bottoms and scattered upland coves.

Features clear streams and beaver ponds, providing vital wetland habitats for migrating waterfowl.

Serves as a habitat for the endangered **Red-cockaded woodpecker

Acts as a demonstration site for wildlife-friendly forest management practices.

CAMPING

Camping Valle Gesso (Entracque): Nestled within the Maritime Alps, Camping Valle Gesso offers a scenic haven for nature enthusiasts. Enveloped by verdant forests and mountain meadows, this campground provides tent and caravan spots alongside rental options like bungalows and chalets. Visitors can partake in hiking, mountain biking, fishing, and more outdoor pursuits, or simply unwind amidst the tranquil mountain vistas.

Camping Royal (Turin): Conveniently situated near Turin's city center, Camping Royal serves as a strategic hub for exploring both urban attractions and Piedmont's natural allure.

With ample space for tents, campers, and caravans, plus diverse rental lodgings such as mobile homes and apartments, this campground ensures a comfortable stay. Guests can avail themselves of amenities like a swimming pool, playground, and restaurant, while also accessing nearby hiking trails, cycling routes, and cultural landmarks.

Camping La Quiete (Lake Maggiore): Positioned along the shores of Lake Maggiore, Camping La Quiete beckons campers seeking a serene lakeside escape. Offering shaded pitches for tents and campers, as well as rental options like bungalows and mobile homes, this campground caters to various preferences. Guests can indulge in swimming, water sports, and leisurely boat excursions on the lake, or explore neighboring towns and attractions such as Stresa, the Borromean Islands, and Villa Taranto's botanical gardens.

Visa and entry requirement

Visa Requirements for Piedmont:

Visa Exemption: Some countries, like the United States, the United Kingdom, and Canada, don't require visas for entry into Piedmont.

Passport Validity: Your passport should remain valid for at least 6 months beyond your planned departure date.

Onward or Return Ticket: You must possess a valid onward or return ticket.

Forms and Documentation:

Upon arrival, travelers need to fill out an immigration form to be presented to an immigration officer.

Visitors are allowed to bring in $1,000 worth of goods duty-free (goods intended to stay in the region).

If you exceed the duty-free limit, you'll need to complete a customs declaration form.

Airlines no longer provide customs forms, so only fill them out if you exceed your duty-free allowance.

Length of Stay:

Visitors can typically stay for up to 90 days, although initially, entry is often granted for 30 days (even if you have a return ticket for a later date).

Extensions to your stay can be arranged by visiting an office of the Immigration Department and paying for an extension.

Transportation Tips

1. By Air: The primary airport serving Piedmont is Turin-Caselle Airport, catering to both domestic and international flights.

It's conveniently located near Turin, the region's capital. If you're arriving by air, this airport is your entry point to Piedmont.

2. By Train: Piedmont boasts a well-connected train network, with high-speed trains linking Turin to major cities like Milan, Bologna, Florence, Rome, and Naples. Traveling by train offers convenience and affordability for exploring the region.

3. Driving: Renting a car is an excellent choice for discovering Piedmont's scenic countryside. Driving along the smaller roads amidst vineyards provides captivating views and a closer look at the grape-growing process. However, be prepared for narrow city streets and limited parking.

4. Local Transportation: While public transportation options within wine country are limited, buses connect towns. For a more flexible and immersive experience, renting a car in Turin and driving to Alba and other towns is recommended.

Safety and Emergency Information

Natural Gas Safety:

If you detect the smell of natural gas or suspect a leak, contact Piedmont at 800.752.7504. For urgent situations, always dial 911.

Utilize Piedmont MyChart to communicate with your doctor for non-emergency concerns.

Emergency Alerts:

Save these numbers in your phone:

Alameda County emergency alerts: (925) 560-5950

City of Piedmont emergency alerts: (510) 420-3000.

Emergency Preparedness:

In case of emergencies, dial 911 (or 9, then 911 from a campus phone) and reach out to Campus Police/Safety for assistance.

Store crucial contact numbers in your phone:

Emergency: Dial 112 (European emergency number) or 911 (if applicable).

Police: Dial 113 (European police emergency number) or 911.

Medical Assistance: Dial 118 (European medical emergency number) or 911.

Fire Department: Dial 115 (European fire emergency number) or 911.

Mountain Safety:

Before embarking on a hike or mountain exploration, adhere to safety protocols:

Inform a trusted individual about your hiking itinerary and anticipated return time.

Carry essential provisions such as water, snacks, a map, and a first aid kit.

Dress appropriately in layers and wear suitable footwear.

Exercise caution around steep inclines, loose rocks, and abrupt weather shifts.

Wildlife Awareness:

Piedmont hosts diverse wildlife; respect their natural habitat and maintain a safe distance.

If you encounter wild animals, refrain from agitating them and refrain from feeding them.

Packing essentials and what to pack for each seasons

1. Autumn (September to November):

Weather: Enjoy mild temperatures and fewer crowds.

What to Bring:

Layered Clothing: Pack lightweight layers suitable for varying temperatures throughout the day.

Sturdy Footwear: Essential for exploring towns and vineyards comfortably.

Rain Gear: Be prepared for occasional showers, especially in October.

Attire for Wine Tasting: Consider semi-formal clothing if you plan to partake in wine tastings.

Truffle Hunting Equipment: If you're visiting during truffle season, bring appropriate gear for truffle hunts.

Weather: Expect cold and damp conditions.

What to Bring:

Warm Layers: Ensure you're bundled up with sweaters, coats, scarves, and gloves.

Waterproof Boots: Necessary for wet weather conditions.

Umbrella: Prepare for frequent rain showers.

Indoor Attire: Dress warmly for indoor activities and visits to wine cellars.

Truffle Season Gear: If you're interested in truffle hunting, pack suitable clothing.

3. Spring (March to May):

Weather: Experience pleasant temperatures and blossoming landscapes.

What to Bring:

Light Layers: Bring a mix of short-sleeve shirts and lightweight jackets.

Comfortable Footwear: Ideal for exploring towns and the countryside.

Sunglasses and Sunscreen: Protect yourself from increasing sun exposure.

Camera: Capture the beauty of spring scenery.

Truffle Season Gear: For truffle enthusiasts, pack accordingly.

4. Summer (June to August):

Weather: Enjoy warm and sunny days.

What to Bring:

Lightweight Clothing: T-shirts, shorts, and dresses are suitable for hot weather.

Sun Hat and Sunglasses: Shield yourself from the sun's rays.

Swimsuit: If you plan to visit lakes or pools.

Comfortable Sandal: Perfect for leisurely walks through charming villages.

Attire for Wine Tasting: Dress comfortably for visits to vineyards.

Truffle Season Gear: For those visiting during truffle season, pack accordingly.

THINGS TO DO DURING PIEDMONT'S SEASONS

Spring: Blossoms and Festivals

In spring, Piedmont bursts into life with a colorful display of blossoms and an array of exciting festivals. As nature awakens from its winter slumber, the region's landscapes are adorned with vibrant flowers, creating picturesque scenes in every corner.

One of the highlights of spring in Piedmont is the blooming of cherry blossoms, which blanket the countryside in delicate shades of pink and white. Visitors can immerse themselves in the beauty of these blossoms by taking leisurely strolls through orchards or picnicking beneath the flowering trees.

Additionally, spring is a time of celebration in Piedmont, with numerous festivals and events taking place throughout the region. From food and wine festivals celebrating the season's bounty to cultural events showcasing local traditions, there's something for everyone to enjoy.

For food enthusiasts, spring brings the opportunity to indulge in fresh produce at markets and food fairs, where seasonal delights such as asparagus, artichokes, and strawberries take center stage. Meanwhile, wine lovers can explore the region's vineyards and participate in tastings to sample the latest vintages.

Cultural festivals abound in spring, offering a glimpse into Piedmont's rich heritage and traditions. Whether it's traditional music and dance performances, historical reenactments, or artisanal craft markets, these events provide a chance to experience the local culture firsthand. spring in Piedmont is a time of renewal and celebration, where nature's beauty is on full display and the region comes alive with the joy of festivals and festivities. It's a perfect season to explore the charms of this enchanting corner of Italy.

Festivals

VINUM: Held in May in Alba, Vinum is a wine festival dedicated to showcasing Piedmont's renowned wines. Visitors can savor wine tastings, join guided tours of local wineries, and indulge in traditional Piedmontese cuisine.

SAGRA DELLE FRAGOLE: Held in April in Nizza Monferrato, this festival marks the beginning of spring and the strawberry harvest. Attendees can enjoy a variety of strawberry-themed dishes, desserts, and beverages, along with engaging activities suitable for all ages.

MAGGIO MUSICALE: Taking place in May in Turin, Maggio Musicale is a month-long music festival featuring performances by both local and international artists. With genres ranging from classical to jazz, the festival offers a diverse selection of musical experiences across the city.

SAGRA DEL TARTUFO: Throughout spring, several towns in Piedmont host truffle festivals, known as "sagre del tartufo," celebrating the esteemed white and black truffles found in the region. These festivals include truffle tastings, cooking demonstrations, truffle hunts, and opportunities to purchase fresh truffles and related products.

FIERA DEL BUE GRASSO: Held in March in Carrù, this traditional festival pays homage to the Piedmontese cattle breed known for its high-quality meat. Visitors can enjoy cattle parades, livestock exhibitions, and culinary contests featuring dishes prepared with the region's renowned "bue grasso" beef.

Summer: Outdoor Excursions

1. Mountain Excursions and Outdoor Dining:

The majestic Alps serve as a breathtaking backdrop for nature enthusiasts.

Put on your hiking boots and explore the picturesque trails, ranging from gentle strolls to more challenging treks.

Prepare a picnic hamper filled with local cheeses, crusty bread, and succulent fruits. Seek out a scenic spot to enjoy your meal amidst the panoramic mountain views.

2. Winery Tours and Vineyard Explorations:

Piedmont is renowned for its expansive vineyards and winemaking heritage. Embark on a guided wine excursion through the rolling hills of the Langhe wine region.

Indulge in tastings of exquisite Barolo, Barbera, and Nebbiolo wines while taking in the sun-kissed landscapes. Don't overlook the opportunity to visit picturesque wine villages like La Morra and Barolo.

3. Discover Turin (Torino):

Turin, the vibrant capital city of Piedmont, thrives during the summer months.

Wander along its refined streets, admire the Baroque and Renaissance architecture, and explore its historic landmarks.

Uncover the city's rich cultural tapestry, including the Duomo di Torino, a 15th-century cathedral adorned with striking Renaissance and Baroque elements.

4. Experience Alba:

Alba beckons to gastronomes with its reputation as a culinary haven. Renowned for its truffles and Langhe wines, this enchanting town offers a sensory feast.

Roam its cobblestone streets, indulge in local specialties like tajarin (egg pasta with shaved truffles), and immerse yourself in the gastronomic pleasures of Piedmont.

5. Savor Lakeside Serenity:

Piedmont boasts enchanting lakes such as Lake Maggiore and Lake Orta. Revel in leisurely boat cruises, swim in the pristine waters, and luxuriate under the sun's rays.

Escape to the tranquil Isola dei Pescatori (Island of the Fishermen) on Lake Maggiore for a serene retreat.

6. Valentino Park in Turin:

Spend a delightful day at Parco del Valentino in Turin. This riverside park offers verdant lawns, meandering pathways, and delightful vistas.

Rent a bicycle, enjoy a picnic, or simply unwind beneath the shade of trees. It's an idyllic setting for outdoor relaxation[8].

Autumn: Harvests and Colors

✓ CRAFTING LEAF WREATHS

Embark on a journey to a peaceful forest, collect golden leaves, and use them to create a seasonal wreath, symbolizing the enchanting beauty of autumn.

✓ EXPLORING CHARMING TOWNS AND CITIES

Alba: Famed for its truffles and Langhe wines, Alba hosts the renowned Alba Truffle Festival. Delight in local specialties like tajarin (egg pasta with shaved truffles) and wander through the picturesque streets.

La Morra: This village offers breathtaking vistas of the Langhe wine region. Stroll amidst vineyards and relish the rolling hills.

✓ WINE TASTING IN THE LANGHE REGION

As autumn ushers in the grape harvest season, explore nearby wineries to savor the exquisite Barolo, Barbera, and Nebbiolo wines amidst vineyards adorned in vibrant red and gold hues, creating a romantic atmosphere for wine enthusiasts.

Truffle Hunting: Immerse yourself in Piedmont's truffle culture by joining a truffle hunt guided by a local expert and their skilled dogs, and feel the thrill of uncovering these earthy treasures nestled beneath the forest floor.

Scenic Fall Foliage Drives: Rent a car and explore the winding roads embraced by vibrant foliage, traversing the Langhe hills and stopping at picturesque viewpoints to appreciate the breathtaking autumn scenery.

Chestnut Festivals: Participate in nearby chestnut festivals (sagre), indulging in roasted chestnuts, chestnut flour dishes, and other seasonal delights, all while celebrating the harvest and the rich flavors of autumn.

Exploring Turin: Immerse yourself in the autumnal charm of Turin as its historic architecture shines brightly. Explore the city's palaces, museums, and elegant squares, ensuring not to miss iconic attractions such as the Royal Palace of Turin and the Egyptian Museum.

Indulging in Comfort Food: Indulge in hearty Piedmontese dishes like brasato al Barolo (beef braised in Barolo wine) and bagna cauda (warm garlic and anchovy dip), and enhance your dining experience with locally sourced wines for a truly authentic culinary adventure.

Winter: Snowy Delights

Winter Sports in Sestriere: For snow enthusiasts, Sestriere offers a prime destination, being one of the earliest purpose-built ski areas globally. Engage in skiing, snowboarding, and other winter activities amidst the stunning Alpine scenery near the French border.

Discover Turin (Torino): Turin, Piedmont's capital city, is an ideal spot for a winter urban getaway. Despite being Italy's fourth-largest city, it remains relatively unexplored by many international travelers.

Explore its historic center, visit landmarks like the Palazzo Reale, Palazzo Madama, and Palazzo Carignano, and delve into the city's rich cultural heritage.

Explore Quaint Towns and Villages: Famed for its truffles and Langhe wines, Alba hosts the renowned Alba White Truffle Fair. Delight in local delicacies and wander through the charming streets.

La Morra: Revel in breathtaking views of the Langhe wine region and rolling hills. Take leisurely strolls through vineyards and soak in the winter atmosphere.

Indulge in Comforting Cuisine: Treat yourself to hearty Piedmontese specialties such as brasato al Barolo (beef braised in Barolo wine) and bagna cauda (a warm garlic and anchovy dip). Accompany your meal with locally sourced wines for an authentic culinary experience.

Winter Hiking and Snowshoeing: Traverse snow-covered landscapes on invigorating winter hikes or snowshoeing excursions. The Alps offer picturesque trails and awe-inspiring vistas, particularly during the serene winter months.

Savor Piedmontese Wine and Chocolate: Embark on tours of local wineries and unwind with a glass of Barolo or Barbera wine. Don't miss the opportunity to indulge in Piedmont's renowned chocolates, especially during the festive holiday season.

Relax by the Fireside: Seek refuge in cozy accommodations complete with fireplaces. Curl up with a good book, savor hot cocoa, and bask in the comforting warmth of Piedmont's hospitality.

SHOPPING AND PRACTICE

Market and locations

Piedmont boasts a diverse array of markets spread across its quaint towns and cities, providing visitors with an enchanting shopping experience.

Here are some noteworthy markets and their locations:

1. TURIN MARKET: Turin, the capital city of Piedmont, hosts multiple markets catering to various interests. Among them is the Porta Palazzo Market, one of Europe's largest open-air markets, offering a wide range of goods from fresh produce to clothing and household items. Other notable markets in Turin include the Balôn flea market, specializing in antiques and vintage items, and the Quadrilatero Romano Market, renowned for its artisanal food products.

2. ALBA MARKET: Alba, famed for its truffles, showcases its reputation through its market scene. Visitors can explore the Alba White Truffle Market, where local truffle hunters and vendors gather to sell fresh truffles and based products.

Additionally, Alba hosts regular farmers' markets featuring the region's seasonal produce and specialty foods.

3. ASTI MARKET: Asti's market scene mirrors the region's viticultural heritage, with the Asti Wine Market being a highlight for wine enthusiasts. Offering a diverse selection of locally produced wines for tasting and purchase, the market is complemented by stalls offering fresh fruits, vegetables, cheeses, and artisanal crafts.

4. BAROLO MARKET: Situated in the Langhe wine region, the town of Barolo is renowned for its namesake wine. Visitors can explore the local market, often featuring wines from nearby vineyards, gourmet food products, and handmade crafts. It's an excellent opportunity to sample regional flavors and acquire distinctive souvenirs.

5. ACQUI TERME MARKET: Acqui Terme's market contributes to the town's charm, alongside its thermal baths and historic architecture.

The Acqui Terme Market offers a diverse range of goods, including local produce, clothing, accessories, and household items. Visitors can leisurely browse through the market stalls, enjoying the lively ambiance of this captivating Italian town.

Bargaining tips

Familiarize Yourself with Italian Phrases: **While English is often understood, knowing some basic Italian phrases can foster a warmer interaction. Greet vendors with a cheerful "Buongiorno" (good morning) or "Buonasera" (good evening).**

Initiate with Courtesy and a Smile: **Approach vendors with a warm smile and courteous manner, as it establishes a positive atmosphere for negotiations. Begin the bargaining process by using phrases such as "Can you offer a better price?" to initiate the discussion.**

Understand Market Values: Research the prevailing prices of the items you wish to purchase to understand the range in the market. Keep abreast of market offerings and trends to make informed decisions.

Consider Bundle Purchases: When purchasing multiple items from the same vendor, contemplate bundling them together. Politely inquire, "Se compro più di uno, mi fai uno sconto?" (If I buy more than one, can you give me a discount?)

Be Prepared to Walk Away: Sometimes, indicating your readiness to walk away can be an effective bargaining tactic. If the price isn't agreeable, express gratitude and politely state, "Grazie, ma è troppo caro" (Thank you, but it's too expensive).

Antique treasure and Artisian crafts

Piedmont Craftsmen

Established in 1963, Piedmont Craftsmen is a guild comprising craft artists and collectors devoted to celebrating handmade objects and conserving the craft heritage of the area.

Representing nearly four hundred skilled artisans across the United States, they showcase both traditional and contemporary craftworks.

Visit their gallery in Winston-Salem, North Carolina, to uncover exquisite craft pieces and engage with talented artists.

Gran Balon and Balon del Sabato

These flea and street markets in Piedmont provide a charming assortment of antiques, vintage discoveries, and unique collectibles.

Explore stalls brimming with clothing, memorabilia, and more. Negotiate with vendors and unearth hidden gems.

Antiq'aria il mercato di Moncalieri

Situated in Moncalieri, this market specializes in antiques. Meander through narrow streets and encounter old-world charm.

From vintage furniture to timeless curiosities, you'll discover something special here.

Bluebird Treasures Thrift Store & Artisan Goods (Bedford, Pennsylvania)

Although not located in Piedmont, this thrift store and artisan goods shop epitomizes the essence of unique discoveries.

Explore their ever-evolving inventory, featuring collectibles and handcrafted items.

Piedmont Craftsmen Fair

Hosted annually in Winston-Salem, this fair brings together over 100 artisans from the Southeast.

Explore a plethora of unique works across various mediums, including clay, wood, glass, fibers, and photography.

Engage with artists, witness demonstrations, and immerse yourself in the world of fine craftsmanship.

Responsible Tourism Initiatives

Responsible tourism efforts in Piedmont are geared towards advocating sustainable travel behaviors and lessening the environmental and cultural impact of tourism.

1. Environmental Protection: Piedmont places great importance on conserving its natural landscapes and biodiversity.

Responsible tourism endeavors concentrate on reducing travelers' ecological footprint by promoting environmentally-friendly activities such as low-impact hiking, wildlife observation, and eco-conscious lodging options.

2. <u>Cultural Conservation:</u> Piedmont boasts a rich cultural heritage, including historic towns, landmarks, and traditional craftsmanship. Responsible tourism initiatives actively work towards preserving local customs and cultural sites by encouraging respectful conduct among visitors, fostering cultural exchange, and backing community-based tourism ventures.

3. <u>Sustainable Lodging:</u> Responsible tourism practices in Piedmont underscore the significance of choosing eco-friendly accommodations. Travelers are encouraged to opt for hotels, guesthouses, and lodges that prioritize sustainability by adopting energy-efficient measures, minimizing waste, and supporting local communities.

4. Community Participation: Responsible tourism endeavors in Piedmont aim to engage local communities in tourism planning and decision-making processes. This involves backing community-owned tourism ventures, advocating for fair wages and working conditions for tourism employees, and nurturing positive interactions between visitors and locals.

5. Education and Awareness: Piedmont encourages travelers to delve into the region's environmental and cultural heritage through educational initiatives, interpretive signage, and guided tours. Responsible tourism initiatives aim to raise awareness about conservation issues, sustainable travel practices, and the significance of preserving Piedmont's distinct identity.

ITINERARY SUGGESTION

DAY 1: ARRIVAL IN TURIN

Fly into Turin-Caselle Airport.

Begin your exploration of Turin:

Visit the historic Royal Palace of Turin to delve into Savoy history.

Stroll through the vibrant Quadrilatero market district to sample local delicacies.

Treat yourself to an authentic Italian dinner at a cozy trattoria.

DAY 2: DISCOVERING TURIN

Spend the day discovering Turin's architectural marvels:

Explore the elegant Palazzo Madama and the majestic Palazzo Carignano.

Wander through the city's lively streets and charming squares.

Indulge in a bicerin, a traditional coffee drink, at one of Turin's historic cafes.

DAY 3: WINE TASTING IN LANGHE

Embark on a full-day wine-tasting tour in the picturesque Lange Hills, renowned for Barolo and Barbaresco wines:

Sample exquisite wines while taking in breathtaking vineyard vistas.

Gain insights into the region's time-honored winemaking traditions.

DAY 4: ALBA AND TRUFFLE HUNTING

Head to Alba, celebrated for its prized truffles:

Join a thrilling white truffle hunting excursion accompanied by a skilled "tabui" dog.

Indulge in a sumptuous truffle-infused meal at a local restaurant.

DAY 5: ASTI AND UNESCO HERITAGE

Explore the UNESCO World Heritage wine region of Asti:

Visit picturesque towns and savor the region's culinary delights.

Immerse yourself in the area's rich cultural heritage.

DAY 6: GASTRONOMIC EXPLORATION

Venture into gastronomic hubs:

Delve deeper into Alba's truffle cuisine.

Explore the neighboring Barbaresco and Barolo wine regions for more epicurean delights.

DAY 7: FAREWELL

Bid adieu to Piedmont:

Reflect on the memorable experiences and cherished moments you've had in this remarkable region.

Depart from Turin-Caselle Airport, carrying with you fond memories of your time in Piedmont.

5day itinerary for nature lovers and romantic getaway

DAY 1: ARRIVAL IN TURIN

Touch down at Turin-Caselle Airport.

Explore the enchanting city of Turin:

Take a leisurely stroll along the banks of the Po River and savor the sunset.

Dine at a charming riverside restaurant.

DAY 2: LANGHE VINEYARDS AND TRUFFLE EXCURSION

Venture into the scenic Langhe region:

Roam through the idyllic vineyards and rolling hills.

Engage in an exhilarating truffle hunting adventure guided by a local expert and their faithful canine companion.

Delight your taste buds with delectable truffle-infused dishes at a cozy eatery.

DAY 3: ALBA AND CULINARY DISCOVERIES

Explore the captivating town of Alba:

Wander along its quaint cobblestone streets.

Explore vibrant local markets and artisan boutiques.

Indulge in the exquisite flavors of Piedmontese cuisine paired with fine wines.

DAY 4: LAKE ORTA AND ROMANTIC BOAT TRIP

Drive to the picturesque Lake Orta:

Discover the charm of Orta San Giulio, a quaint lakeside town.

Embark on a romantic boat excursion across the tranquil waters of the lake.

Enjoy a candlelit dinner with a mesmerizing view of the lake.

DAY 5: SACRO MONTE DI CREA AND SUNSET SERENITY

Journey to Sacro Monte di Crea:

Trek up to the sanctuary perched atop the hill.

Marvel at the panoramic vistas of the surrounding countryside.

Witness a breathtaking sunset together, creating lasting memories of your romantic getaway in Piedmont.

5 day itinerary for family adventure

➤ DAY 1: ARRIVAL IN TURIN

Turin

Arrive at Turin-Caselle Airport.

Explore the city:

Visit the Royal Palace of Turin to delve into Savoy history.

Take a leisurely walk along the banks of the Po River and enjoy the sunset.

Dine at a cozy restaurant nestled by the riverside.

➢ DAY 2: LANGHE VINEYARDS AND TRUFFLE HUNTING

Langhe Region:

Venture into the picturesque vineyards and rolling hills.

Join a truffle hunting expedition led by a local guide and their faithful dog.

Indulge in delectable dishes infused with truffles at a quaint restaurant.

➢ DAY 3: ALBA AND CULINARY DELIGHTS

Alba:

Wander through the charming cobblestone streets.

Explore the vibrant local markets and artisan boutiques.

Treat yourself to the flavors of Piedmontese cuisine accompanied by fine wines.

> ## Day 4: Lake Orta and Family Fun

Lake Orta:

Discover the enchanting lakeside town of Orta San Giulio.

Enjoy a family-friendly boat excursion on the tranquil lake.

Have a delightful picnic by the water's edge.

> ## Day 5: Sacro Monte di Crea and Outdoor Activities

Sacro Monte di Crea:

Embark on a hike to reach the hilltop sanctuary.

Marvel at the sweeping panoramic vistas of the surrounding countryside.

Engage in family-friendly outdoor pursuits such as birdwatching or leisurely nature walks.

Day 1: Turin - Culinary Hub of Piedmont

Morning: Arrive in Turin and kick off your culinary journey with a classic Italian breakfast at a nearby café, enjoying espresso and freshly baked pastries.

Midday: Explore Turin's vibrant food markets like the Porta Palazzo Market, where you can sample local cheeses, cured meats, and fresh produce.

Afternoon: Join a guided food tour of Turin to sample regional delights such as agnolotti pasta, bagna cauda (a warm garlic and anchovy dip), and gianduja chocolate.

Evening: Indulge in Piedmontese favorites like brasato al Barolo (beef braised in Barolo wine) and vitello tonnato (veal with tuna sauce) at a traditional trattoria or osteria.

Day 2: Alba - Home of Truffle Delicacies

Morning: Journey to Alba, famous for its truffles, and explore the Alba White Truffle Market during truffle season to experience the excitement of truffle auctions.

Midday: Delight in a truffle-infused lunch at a local restaurant, savoring dishes like tajarin pasta with shaved white truffles or fonduta with truffle.

Afternoon: Wander through Alba's charming streets and visit artisanal shops offering a variety of truffle-infused products such as oils, cheeses, and condiments.

Evening: Treat yourself to a gourmet dinner at a Michelin-starred restaurant in Alba, where innovative dishes made with locally sourced, seasonal ingredients await.

Day 3: Langhe Wine Region - Vineyards and Cellars

<u>Morning:</u> Embark on a wine tour of the Langhe region, exploring renowned wineries like Barolo and Barbaresco to sample exceptional wines like Barolo, Barbera, and Nebbiolo.

<u>Midday:</u> Enjoy a leisurely lunch at a winery restaurant, pairing Piedmontese wines with delectable dishes such as carne cruda (beef tartare) or vitello tonnato.

<u>Afternoon:</u> Take in the breathtaking views of the Langhe's vineyards and hilltop villages while exploring the picturesque countryside.

<u>Evening:</u> Conclude your day with a wine tasting dinner at a family-operated agriturismo, where you can relish traditional dishes crafted with fresh, seasonal ingredients paired with local wines.

Day 4: Asti - Gastronomic Traditions and Festivals

Morning: Travel to Asti and visit the local farmers' market to discover an array of seasonal produce, artisanal cheeses, and cured meats.

Midday: Enjoy a leisurely lunch at a trattoria in Asti, feasting on regional specialties like bagna cauda, agnolotti del plin (meat-filled pasta), and Asti spumante risotto.

Afternoon: Explore the historic center of Asti, taking in landmarks like the Cathedral of Santa Maria Assunta and the Torre Troyana.

Evening: If your visit coincides with festival season, immerse yourself in the local food culture by attending a food festival like the Festival delle Sagre Astigiane, where you can sample a variety of traditional Piedmontese dishes and delicacies.

CONCLUSION

In Northern Italy lies a region that enchants with its natural splendor, cultural heritage, and culinary mastery. Piedmont, often revered as the "Land of Slow Food," promises a unique journey where each moment unfolds like a chapter in an eternal story. As you traverse the rolling landscapes of Piedmont, you are greeted by vineyards stretching to the horizon and majestic peaks crowned with snow. Here, nature's beauty isn't just a backdrop but an integral part of the region's essence, beckoning you to immerse yourself in its serene ambiance.

Yet, Piedmont's allure extends beyond its picturesque scenery; it is a treasure trove of history waiting to be explored. From the opulence of Turin's royal palaces to the quaint charm of medieval towns like Alba and Asti, the echoes of the past resonate through cobblestone streets and ancient walls, weaving tales of bygone eras.

However, the true magic of Piedmont lies in its culinary heritage. Here, food isn't just sustenance but a celebration of life itself – a harmonious symphony of flavors that tantalize the taste buds and awaken the senses. From the elusive white truffles of Alba to the bold wines of the Langhe, Piedmont's gastronomy is a testament to its dedication to excellence and tradition. In Piedmont, every meal is a celebration, a homage to the land and the artisans who craft its bounty. Whether relishing a plate of agnolotti del plin or sipping on a glass of velvety Barolo, each bite tells a story steeped in centuries-old recipes and a profound connection to the land.

Yet, Piedmont offers more than just culinary delights; it fosters a sense of community and connection. Here, strangers become friends over shared meals and shared experiences, reminding us of the importance of slowing down and savoring life's simple pleasures.

As you bid adieu to Piedmont, carry along with you not only memories of its breathtaking landscapes and delectable cuisine but also the lessons it imparts. May we remember to cherish each moment, to embrace the beauty of simplicity, and to recognize the interconnectedness of all things. InPiedmont, you find not just a destination but a way of life – one that nourishes the body, delights the soul, and celebrates the essence of being alive.

Made in United States
North Haven, CT
08 June 2025

69617191R00108